DREAM JOURNEY, BREAKING THE DREAM BARRIERS™

DREAM JOURNEY, BREAKING THE DREAM BARRIERS™

A GUIDE TO BRIDGING IDENTITY GAPS IN LIFE AND CAREER

GEORGIA LEE ARTS
CERTIFIED COACH

Library of Congress Cataloging-in-Publication Data
ISBN: 979-8-218-53429-5 (Paperback)
ISBN: 979-8-218-53428-8 (eBook)

For my family and supporters who lifted me up,
enabling me to help others in return, with gratitude

CONTENTS

WARRIOR OF THE HEART

To the Land of Elysian Dream I sail,
Where courage rises like dawn's first gleam,
For from the heart the bold take flight,
The place where precious dreams crystallize in light.

Fear whispers like a thief in the night,
A dream killer, shadow cloaked in fright,
But the warrior knows, deep in the chest,
That courage is born where the heart finds rest.

On this journey through skies unknown,
I face the storms that howl and moan,
But each drop that falls, a diamond's gleam,
Rains down on the path to my Elysian Dream.

For every battle fought with love's embrace,
Is a step toward a sacred, unyielding place,
Where heart and hope become one flame,
And fear, no longer, has a name.

With every beat, the rhythm is clear,
The heart's true voice speaks louder than fear.
And in the land where dreams take form,
The warrior's heart becomes the storm.

Raining diamonds, the future unfolds,
A vision bright, in the soul it molds,
For in the heart, we find the way,
To an Elysian Dream that will forever stay.

So, onward, with the heart as guide,
Through valleys deep and mountains wide,
The warrior's journey, fierce and true,
Is the dream that lives within you.

INTRODUCTION

Dream Journey, Breaking the Dream Barriers™ is a journey into "a magical transformational dreamscape where adorned warriors take a Hero /Heroine's journey as the artist of their dreams. Where Your Precious Dreams Crystallize with Diamond Rain and Diamond Dreams, **the Elysian Dream philosopher's stone™**". It is a journey into the heart of chaos, where you crystallize your dreams. Fear is a number one dream killer. It takes courage to overcome fear. Courage is derived from the word heart. As a warrior of your heart, you will find the courage that you need to slay your dragons so you can get to victory. In Greek mythology, Khaos was the first being or entity to exist in the formless void that preceded the creation of the universe. Chaos, derived from the Greek word 'Khaos,' is a cataclysmic gap – a deep chasm of nothingness. A gap is a break in the barrier where there is an opening between two things, and victory is just on the other side, but first, you must figure out how to get there.

Think of this gap as an adventure to optimize your life and reclaim your energy, wellness, and dreams, whether you have small dreams that keep you Earthbound or stellar-sized dreams that launch you to the moon. You can find your path, life purpose, and meaning.

Imagine a rocket named the "Dream Journey ™". Its mission is to help earthlings "Break the Dream Barriers" ™ by transcending the IDENTITY GAP. Now, imagine that you see a portal or door in front of you, which is a gateway to a liminal dreamscape called The Land of Dreams. It is a transitory place, where you are a warrior on a hero or heroine's journey, who is in-between identities. You are not who you were, and you are not yet who you are becoming. Before liftoff, the rocket is grounded on a launch pad, like we are in our everyday lives, anchored by routines, roles, and expectations. Liminal spaces are like the moment a rocket launches from Earth, leaving the familiar behind and entering an otherworldly place on a mission of discovery. But in the process of growth, we must move through a liminal phase— the transitional period where the old is left behind, and the new is not yet realized. As the rocket ascends, it must pass through layers of the atmosphere, like we push through uncertainty, discomfort, and fear in our own transformations. These layers can be turbulent, testing our resolve and courage. However, just as the rocket uses the force of gravity to propel itself forward, we too can harness the weight of our doubts and challenges to fuel our growth.

The rocket reaches space—an expansive, unknown territory— like the space of possibility that lies on the other side of our transformation. In this liminal, everything is potential; we become explorers, navigating our inner landscapes, recalibrating our identity, and crystallizing our goals. Just as the rocket follows its mission, we emerge from the liminal phase with clarity, ready to pursue our new path with purpose and direction.

You may feel like the protagonist in Robert A. Heinlein's story, "Stranger in a Strange Land," who's a Martian who moves to Earth. In this liminal space, you may feel lost, alone, confused, uncomfortable, empty, stuck, or afraid. In this liminal space, it may seem eerie, empty, surreal, or like an abandoned place. This space is your blank canvas where you are like an artist, and you can create the life you want by transforming your story, building a new world, being curious, developing your awareness, and developing new habits so you can create your next best self. In this space, you can also reclaim your energy, wellness, and dreams so you can live a valuable life.

There is a natural polarity in liminal spaces, as they exist in a state of tension between opposing forces or states of being. When your career and life are balanced, it can feel like a blissful, peaceful paradise. Everything is dual, a pair of opposites. Liminality, by definition, is the threshold between what was and what will be, and this inherently creates a space of duality or polarity. When you find balance in the polarities, you find flow. Here are key polarities present in liminal spaces:

Order and Chaos: In liminal spaces, we often experience both the comfort of structure and the unpredictability of change. As we transition, we leave behind the familiar order of our old identity or situation and enter the chaotic, uncertain potential of what could be. This is where you harness the power of cosmic creation, like an artist with a blank canvas, to create your beautiful life. Cosmos, a Greek word for the order of the universe, is the opposite of chaos.

"In all chaos there is a cosmos. In all disorder there is a secret disorder…this is the archetype of meaning, just as the anima is the archetype of life itself." – CARL JUNG

Fear and Hope: Liminal spaces can evoke fear because of the unknown, but they also hold hope for what is to come. This polarity creates a push and pull, where we may feel anxious about letting go of the past yet simultaneously excited for the future.

Old and New Identity: In liminality, there is the tension between the person we were and the person we are becoming. Our old identity is still present, but an updated version of ourselves is forming, creating a space of inner conflict and potential growth.

Stagnation and Transformation: While we can feel stuck or suspended in liminal spaces, this is also the place where profound transformation happens. The polarity between feeling static and the potential for movement and change is what makes liminal spaces so powerful.

These polarities make liminal spaces rich environments for personal growth, as they force us to confront opposites, integrate dualities, and move beyond into new states of being.

The number one regret people have at the end of life is that they didn't live the life of their dreams. You can't chase the right dream if you are stuck in the gap. Just like a countdown timer for a rocket launch, time is running out, and the time to get out of the gap is now.

You can listen to our podcast, Dream Journey, Breaking the Dream Barriers™, at elysiandream.net.

A STUNNING DRESS
MADE OF HELLFIRE...

She wore her scars as her best attire.
A stunning dress made of hellfire.

Lines are written across her face.
More than just a little trace.

Her beauty comes from deep inside.
She never turns her face to hide.

She stays aware, she's super cool.
This woman is nobody's fool.

Spit at her, and she'll spit right back.
You'll never knock her off the track.

She's been around the block it's true.
More than let's say me and you.

She's seen it all a thousand times.
Paid attention, read the signs.

Been right there and done it all.
Now she's back and walking tall.

Not afraid to get it wrong.
Play the song, she'll sing along.

Lines are written across her face.
More than just a little trace.

She wore her scars as her best attire.
A stunning dress made of hellfire.

LOUIS D'ALTO

CHAPTER 1
IDENTITY THEFT

Career Chaos

Have you ever felt like you were tumbling down a rabbit hole, unsure of your career path or life purpose? It's much like that famous quote from *Alice in Wonderland*: "I knew who I was this morning, but I've changed a few times since then." If that resonates with you, it's because you're experiencing what I call the *IDENTITY GAP*. Life is full of transitions—whether you're a college-bound student, a mid-career professional, a transitioning veteran, an entrepreneur, or approaching retirement. With each stage, your identity needs to shift and evolve.

Here's the thing: if you don't pivot your identity with these changes, you risk stagnation—a slow death of the soul. Even worse, if you fail to pivot in your career, you could find yourself at the bottom of burnout or exhausted from a toxic job and unable to work. If you don't have an income, then you can lose everything that you hold dear. One of the biggest regrets people have at the end of their lives is not living the life of their dreams and not creating a legacy. You may be in the middle of a great life story, but if you're not actively thinking about your next chapter, you'll get stuck.

Consider this: you spend about one-third of your life working. If your career isn't aligned with your true self, it impacts everything—your health, relationships, and even your sleep. Unfortunately, many people find themselves stuck in jobs they hate, weighed down by student loans, mortgages, credit card debt, and a lack of a clear dream to chase. This misalignment can lead to anxiety, depression, and burnout. If you're living someone else's story—whether it's following a career path to please your parents or sticking with choices that no longer reflect your true self— you're not really living. How can you chase the right dream if you don't know who you are?

When it comes to identity, some people lack the right tools for growth and self-discovery. Others lack a stable core of self-identity, struggle with self-reflection, and exhibit a deficit in empathy. This latter type is what I call an *identity vampire*—a dream grinch— who drains your energy, leaving you lifeless and erased as they attempt to become you. Sadly, while this type of individual requires professional help, effective treatments are often lacking.

Erased by Father: Descent into Chaos

My downfall began when I transitioned from a professional part of my career into a dysfunctional, male-dominated, discriminatory environment. My career counseling was less about professional development and more about men's deeply ingrained fear that a woman's womb is a national security threat. I was threatened with termination if I became a mother and was told I deserved to lose my home and savings. Women, I was told, belonged at home and were routinely body shamed. My benefits, including sick leave, vacation, and retirement, were stripped because I was expected to get those from my husband. Financially forced to retrain, I found myself back on shift work, unable to attend night classes for my degrees in psychology, social work, and art.

As I climbed the ranks of military leadership, I co-led and led missions where precision was critical, but my authority was constantly undermined—especially as a woman. Reflecting on tragedies like the 1994 Blackhawk Shootdown, which resulted in twenty-six deaths due to friendly fire, only deepened my awareness of how leadership failures can have devastating consequences. The 90s was a cataclysmic time in my career as I learned about the fragility of life when we lost one AWACS aircrew shortly after takeoff when the engines ingested migrating birds. Twenty-four crewmembers lost their lives. I lived a few miles from the Oklahoma City Bombing when Timothy McVeigh and Terry Nichols exploded the bomb that killed 168 people. Life can be over in the blink of an eye. The Air Force values of Integrity First, Service Before Self, and Excellence in All We Do exist for a reason.

Becoming a whistleblower marked the end of my career. No one plans to become a whistleblower; it is a moral dilemma that you find yourself in. Though I had shattered the glass ceiling, I soon found myself standing on a glass cliff, in a position designed to fail. My attempts to pivot or progress in my career were blocked at every turn. In the dehumanizing environment that I worked in, my superiors stripped me of my identity through coercive control. I was beyond burnout and found myself mentally checking out. It was like being a deer, frozen in the headlights, unable to get out of the way. It was too late to pivot.

I found myself lost in what I now call the *IDENTITY GAP*. Failing to pivot, I almost didn't survive. My professional identity was stolen, and my achievements erased. I was dehumanized and erased not just in my career but of who I was—professionally and as a woman. I was criminally drugged—without informed consent— before testifying against corrupt powers that perpetuated physical, psychological, and emotional abuse. There was a medical conflict of interest in my case, and one person was removed, but that influence remained. Years later, I would discover that these drugs erased parts of my memory and identity and caused lasting damage.

From 2007 to 2024, I couldn't obtain proper medical care through allopathic medicine. Doctors don't understand that shiftwork is an occupational hazard. They may overlook sleep deprivation, circadian rhythm, workplace abuse and violence, burnout, chronic fatigue syndrome, the eight dimensions of wellness, or hormone imbalance. Doctors don't see a professional woman who needs a lifestyle change, but hysteria. Medical errors are a leading cause of death. The miracle I found to help me reclaim my life was Functional Medicine Doctors.

In this void, I experienced the *Dark Night of the Soul*, a term Carl Jung used to describe the lowest depths of despair and confusion. It was a time when my soul felt utterly lost, and I questioned everything which I had once believed. What I learned in that dark place is that our perception shapes our reality. I grew up in a household where my parents treated each other as equals, so I was unaware of the inequalities that exist in many workplaces. The role and value of motherhood evolved during the women's rights movement and World War II, as women entered the workforce to fill the roles left by men who went off to war, symbolized by the iconic image of Rosie the Riveter. Despite these changes, I found myself trapped in the cognitive dissonance between my upbringing and the programs supporting women. The glossy posters promoting workplace rights and the polished marketing efforts were deceptive, masking the harsh reality of my toxic work environment. Blindly trusting systems meant to help me nearly cost me everything. However, my disillusionment wasn't limited to male-dominated spaces.

Erased by Mother: Descent into Chaos

Once you fall, it's hard to get up. After transitioning from the military, I expected to regain my health and rebuild my career. But the betrayal I faced was deeper than I could have imagined. Women I trusted to support me chose to uplift the hero—the men—over me, the antihero. My medical providers, upset that my testimony was upheld, attempted to fabricate diagnoses to cover up the criminal prescriptions. They falsified records, felony drugging, while the system I trusted to heal me mirrored the toxic environment I had left behind. I was dumped as a patient and left to die without explanation. It took seven years from the time I was first informed of the criminal prescriptions to see through the gaslighting because of the cognitive dissonance in trusting doctors. The initial prescriber had a prior history of criminal conviction as a doctor. I could spend the rest of my life seeking justice or expose the cover-up and tell the world.

A Facebook group helped me discover the truth about the prescriptions that I was given and helped save my life. I suffered, abandoned and alone, as if I were a participant in the Hunger Games, an experiment. How could I get off the glue trap and not die?

The hardest part was not the male-dominated space, but the grief caused by being let down by other women—those in leadership, transition services, nonprofits, and business development services—who saw me as someone to capitalize on and as a competition rather than a collaborative partner. Behind their public façade of empathy and support for veterans, I witnessed cruelty and greed that kept veterans invisible, powerless, and dependent. Imagine spending more than a decade trying to rise instead of a few short months. In many women's groups that I attended, the leader would be the 'queen bee' with a group that was disempowered, drugged, and dependent.

As I fought to rise, I entered a pattern of relational aggression from women. The years—over a decade—of struggling to rebuild wasn't just due to inadequate healthcare; it was also due to the relational aggression from women in positions of power who failed to advocate for others and, as a result, enslave and disempower them. The issue wasn't a lack of resources; it was a lack of genuine humanity and respect for other women. This is why I nearly ended up homeless, in deep high-interest medical and living expense debt, and why I gained a deep understanding of the 22-veterans-a-day tragedy. When you lose your health, wealth, and purpose and are beat down by women whose job it is to support you, there isn't much left.

During this time, I found work in minimum-wage positions, only to be excluded from opportunities because of others' insecurities. In one case, I relocated to a job only to find out the office manager felt threatened and rescinded the offer. Another nonprofit canceled my volunteer role, which would have led to a paying position because I refused to hand over my program. When you work in low-level positions, there is noticeably less aggression. I then began an entrepreneurial program to start my dream business. A mentor, my instructor's business partner, told me I didn't have the right to my ideas or business plan. She was sharing it with other coaches and empowered them to use my creation. When I asked for respect and support to help me rise, it was denied. My business was hazed, and these coaches would plant a new friend or networking partner in my group to compete, and my business nearly failed. I found myself paying for trademarks so I could work in my community. Most women's empowerment and wellness programs are a form of disempowerment.

The real slap in the face was my failure to identify a top competitor sitting next to me in class. She was in a private networking group with my instructor—a group from which I was excluded. In another collaborative networking group, I tried to create a collaboration which was denied. I thought her business was about helping women with their finances, but then she later advertised as a career coach and a platform hosting multiple coaches—all using my story and trying to tell women how to break barriers, the pay gap, women's empowerment, identity, and toxic work environments. Their greed, desperation for the spotlight, and need to dominate their actions show they cannot empower any woman.

The same veterans' leaders who canceled me in the years prior and wanted to take credit for my program would pivot in front of me, using my creation to get credit in the veteran community. Many of these leaders do not support women rising in their visibility and power, but contribute to homeless and the tragic statistical 22 a day. Sometimes, I feel sick watching women in community leadership positions, knowing that they are driving the very issue they proclaim to solve.

Yet another coach I reached out to for potential collaboration began competing with my business instead of supporting me. When I asked her to level up, I found myself canceled. I received a cease-and-desist order threatening me with arrest if I network my business. Then began the online smear campaign and being canceled by her supporters.

As hard as these women tried to drive me to the street, just another expendable veteran to capitalize on, I rose. When you are authentic in your story, your character, and your business, it will shine through any adversity. When you are secure in your being and aligned in your energy, you don't have to dominate, capitalize on others at their expense, or chase people or businesses. When you align your identity compass with who you are and feel good about yourself, then it will help you maintain a course of true north, which will help you attract the ideal people and clients. Frauds may have short-term success, but if you have a fake persona, harm others, or are just an opportunist, then know that your identity compass can only lead you to eventual failure and that your credibility will be destroyed. Applying the principles of yin and yang to this, think about how the sun compliments the earth and how they don't need to compete with one another. Stepping into another woman's power whose identity is aligned is like trying to put out Star Wars with a firehose, which is impossible.

From SERE to Thriving: The Skills That Saved My Life

What helped me through extreme adversity—and kept me from becoming one of the tragic twenty-two veterans who take their own lives each day—wasn't just luck. It was the training I received in the early '90s at SERE (Survival, Evasion, Resistance, and Escape) training. SERE taught me how to survive in enemy territory and endure the harshest conditions of a simulated prisoner of war camp, but those skills go far beyond the battlefield. They became invaluable tools for surviving the battles of everyday life— physical, mental, and emotional. I learned resilience, the ability to adapt under pressure, and resourcefulness in the face of limited options. Grit and perseverance kept me going when giving up felt easier. Leadership and teamwork taught me the value of relying on others and helping them do the same. But I held onto the belief in a higher power that gave me strength when mine ran out.

These principles—survival, resilience, adaptability, and faith— are what saved me. They transformed my ability to face life's toughest challenges head-on. Today, they continue to serve as a reminder that no matter how overwhelming the odds are, the will to survive is stronger.

From Chaos to Victory: Elysian Dream YOUniversity

Failure hurts, and you have two options: You can either hide in the shadows of your pain, or you can examine the failure, learn from it, and learn how you can help others avoid the same mistake. I discovered IDENTITY GAP in the market in 2015 after being denied critical transition services to restore my health and professional identity after my failure to pivot and collapse. Elysian Dream™ was realized in 2022. It is a metaphor in Greek mythology. "Elysian" is an exclusive, blissful, peaceful paradise where heroes and heroines go after a lengthy battle to reclaim lost pieces of IDENTITY and find peace. Within the world of Elysian is a place called the Land of Dreams.

Learning the art of the pivot and getting the right healthcare are critical to maintaining career wellness. Part of my failure was not pivoting despite red flags; then, it was too late to pivot. The other part of my collapse was due to a lack of understanding of women's healthcare. With my experience in helping people develop professional identity dating back to the mid-90s, I knew what I needed, but that service was denied. I didn't just survive identity theft; I thrived through it and rose, wearing a stunning hellfire dress. From the ashes of my experience came a life and career transitions program designed for people like you—whether you're a student, mid-career professional, veteran, or someone looking to reinvent themselves.

My why and my mission is to help others pivot to stay out of and get out of the IDENTITY GAP before it's too late and avoiding the biggest regret of all—not living the life of their dreams. Life is too short to stay stuck. Doing work that aligns with who you are is a critical part of wellness. You deserve to wake up every day with passion, purpose, and a career that fulfills you. If you are stuck in a toxic environment, then let me help you pivot, go from surviving to thriving, and take all of the stones cast at you to help you rewrite your trauma narrative so you can create a new chapter in your life.

In addition to helping people develop and reinvent their professional identity, I have coached clients from foreign countries who want to develop an individual identity and a sense of self outside others, adoptees, men, women, veterans, and college-bound students. I have also worked with people to restore masculine and feminine polarity so they can experience wholeness in their identity, energy, and in their relationships.

Elysian Dream YOUniversity is not just about career coaching—it's a career wellness sanctuary that is about holistic transformation through *Deep Space Identity Coaching*. It blends proven scientific methods, narrative, depth, metaphors, language, creative thinking, liminality, the hero/heroine's journey, energy, masculine and feminine polarity, and dream coaching to help you align your life and career with who you truly are. In the sanctuary, you are valued, heard, seen, appreciated, validated, understood, and respected. Entering the void of self-discovery is not just about changing jobs or finding new goals—it's about tapping into your deepest identity and living your true purpose. Most people spend their lives chasing the wrong dream. My mission is to help you tap into your identity so you can chase the fight dream, artfully pivot through life's inevitable transitions, and avoid the regret of not living the life you deserve. In short, I sell dreams!

Elysian Dream is "a magical transformational dreamscape where adorned warriors take a Hero / Heroine's journey as the artist of their dreams. Where Your Precious Dreams Crystallize with Diamond Rain and Diamond Dreams, **the Elysian Dream philosopher's stone ™ "**.

Your Dreams Awaits

If you're ready to pivot, redefine your identity, and start living the life you truly desire, Elysian Dream YOUniversity is here to help. This book offers a glimpse into the tools we provide, but the real transformation happens when you dive deeper with

Elysian Dream YOUniversity. For personalized guidance and lasting change, visit elysiandream.net and take the first step toward mastering the art of the pivot.

Now that we've explored the painful experience of *identity theft*, where pieces of who you are get stripped away by conditioning and external forces, let's shift our focus to "**the IDENTITY GAP**". While identity theft can feel like a sudden and shocking loss, the IDENTITY GAP is more subtle, a void that grows over time. It's the space between who you are and who you want to become. This gap can leave you feeling stuck, unfulfilled, and questioning your purpose. But it's also an opportunity—a chance to pivot, reclaim your power, and align your life with your true self. Remember, to master the art of the pivot, you first need to understand the IDENTITY GAP. So now, let's dive deeper into the *IDENTITY GAP* and how to navigate it.

CHAPTER 2
THE IDENTITY GAP

Imagine floating at the edge of a vast, unfamiliar dreamscape in the void of outer space. On Earth, the ground beneath you was firm, solid, defined by the roles you've played and the identity you've built over the years. But just ahead, the terrain shifts—softens—into something unknown.

You meet your future self, a Martian, who's your guide on a journey into transformation. You sit across from each other in a glowing, crystalline room. Communication devices hum softly in the background. The Martian emits a series of bleeps and beeps while you, the human, nervously glance at a translation tablet that is malfunctioning.

Martian (bleeping softly):

"Bleep, bleep…IDENTITY, 55%, 14%, #1, 99%, 40%, 20%, 50%, 47% Beep beep."

Human (confused but trying to stay calm):

"Uh… right. So, I'm guessing that means… 'Hello'?"

Martian (with a final, harmonious beep):

"Bleep beep bloop… GAP, 89%, 44%, 65%, 1/3, bloop, beep."

Human (closing the dialogue): Dream Journey, Breaking the Dream Barriers™

"Language alchemy… it is about teaching earthlings how to understand the IDENTITY GAP so they can avoid it and escape it. Being in the IDENTITY GAP is like being on an otherworldly adventure to a far-away planet with a different language. You must explore your deep spaces to get out of the gap so you can avoid the number one regret that you didn't live the life of your dreams. Most earthlings are living a low-quality life. 55% of earthlings identity is doing work that aligns with who you are. Only 14% are thriving and experiencing optimal happiness. A number one regret is not living the life of your dreams. 99% of college students choose the wrong studies, and 40% regret their choice of majors. Only 20% like the work they do, and 50% lack purpose and meaning at work. 47% of mid-career professionals feel they made the wrong career choice and are stuck with student loans, credit cards, and now have a family, so they feel stuck in their career and end up depressed, feeling hopeless about the future, and turn to prescriptions as the solution. Up to 89% feel burned out at work. 44% of veterans struggle with pivoting their identity, and 65% feel disconnected from civilian life. Earthlings spend one-third of their life working. Then, they find themselves trapped in a career they don't like and don't have a work-life balance. Being in the wrong career and not having a work-life balance impacts the one-third of life spent sleeping which then impairs the final one-third of life."

IDENTITY GAP MISSION: *Close the IDENTITY GAP by helping earthlings live a high-quality life by providing education and resources for identity development in life and career.*

They share a moment of silence, both glowing in their new-found connection through the magic of language alchemy. This is the IDENTITY GAP—it's like learning a foreign language. The space where who you were no longer aligns with who you're becoming. It's the disorienting moment when the labels and roles that once fit so well begin to feel like clothes that have shrunk in the wash. Whether you're transitioning from a long-held career, stepping into a new life chapter, or simply feeling the tug of change in your core, the IDENTITY GAP challenges everything you thought you knew about yourself.

This guide is your map for navigating that uncertain terrain. It's about more than just finding your way; it's about redefining what your identity means in a world that's constantly shifting like quicksand beneath your feet. We'll explore why the IDENTITY GAP happens, how it can leave you feeling lost or unmoored, and, most importantly, how you can bridge this gap to emerge not just intact but more authentically you than ever before. If you've ever felt like the person you're becoming is just out of reach, this guide is for you. Together, we'll traverse the gap and discover the new, expansive identity waiting on the other side.

Understanding the IDENTITY GAP

The first step to navigating the IDENTITY GAP is to understand what identity is and why it's important to remember as you pivot through life. Your identity is not static; it's a dynamic part of who you are. It includes the qualities, beliefs, personality traits, expressions, and roles that define you as an individual. Identity encompasses how you see yourself and how you are recognized by others. It can include aspects like gender, ethnicity, culture, profession, social roles, and personal values. Identity is both a personal construct and a social phenomenon shaped by individual experiences and societal influences.

"Know thyself." – SOCRATES

Now, imagine waking up one morning feeling like a stranger in your own life. The job that once brought you joy now feels meaningless. Your relationships seem distant, and you can't shake the feeling that something is profoundly off, even though everything on the surface appears fine. This unsettling sense of disconnection is more than just a difficult day; it's a warning sign of an IDENTITY GAP—a silent crisis that slowly erodes your sense of self, leaving you questioning who you are and where you belong.

What is the IDENTITY GAP? An IDENTITY GAP is when you feel stuck, lost, or confused. It's a deep chasm that forms when the life you're living no longer aligns with the person you believe yourself to be. It's the gnawing doubt that creeps in when you're faced with major life transitions—whether it's a new career, a significant loss, or the sudden realization that your dreams no longer fit your reality. This gap can manifest in ways that are easy to overlook but impossible to ignore: chronic anxiety, social withdrawal, a loss of motivation, and an overwhelming sense of uncertainty about the future.

"The most common form of despair is not being who you are."
– SOREN KIERKEGAARD

The IDENTITY GAP refers to the dissonance or disconnect between your current identity and the identity required or desired in a new life stage or career phase. This gap manifests when your self-concept—formed by past experiences, roles, and social expectations—no longer aligns with the demands, challenges, or opportunities presented by a transition.

For example, a professional who has dedicated years to a particular career might struggle to redefine themselves when faced with a job loss, career change, or retirement. Similarly, a person moving from a long-term relationship into singlehood or transitioning from military to civilian life may experience an IDENTITY GAP as they grapple with the shift in roles and the loss of a previous identity.

Why Understanding Your Identity Matters

What is Identity? Identity is more than just a collection of characteristics, traits, beliefs, and experiences. It's the essence of who you are, shaping how you see yourself and your place in the world. While foundational and intrinsic identity is not fixed; it evolves over time, influenced by gender, culture, values, roles, personal history, and how you relate to others. Your identity might include being a woman, a man, a veteran, an artist, a parent, a citizen of a certain country, or someone who holds specific values or beliefs.

Understanding your identity is foundational to leading a fulfilling and purpose-driven life. When you truly know who you are, you make choices that align with your authentic self, leading to greater satisfaction in every area of life. Without a clear understanding of your identity, you might find yourself living according to others' expectations, societal norms, or outdated beliefs that no longer serve you. This disconnect can lead to frustration, confusion, and an underlying feeling that something is missing.

By taking the time to explore and understand the various facets of your identity, you not only gain clarity but also unlock the ability to shape your future. This self-awareness allows you to navigate life's challenges more effectively, make empowered choices, and live with greater intention. Your identity is like a compass that guides you toward the life you desire, but only if you understand how to read it.

Imagine Your Identity as a Multifaceted Gem

Think of your identity as a sparkling gem, with each facet representing a different aspect of who you are—your roles, values, beliefs, passions, and relationships. What if you could adjust these facets to shine brighter and align more closely with your true self and life goals?

Understanding the various facets that make up your identity can offer profound insights into personal growth and help bridge any IDENTITY GAPs. Here are the key facets to consider:

- **Personal Identity:** The essence of who you are, shaped by your values, beliefs, and life experiences.

- **Self-Concept:** Your perception of yourself, including self-esteem and self-worth.

- **Values and Beliefs:** The core principles that guide your behavior and decisions.

- **Personality Traits:** Patterns of thinking, feeling, and behaving that define you.

- **Social Identity:** Your membership in various groups and how others perceive you.

- **Cultural Identity:** Belonging to a specific culture, ethnicity, traditions, and language.

- **Gender and Sexual Identity:** Your experience of gender and sexual orientation.

- **Professional Identity:** How you view yourself within your career or profession.

- **Relational Identity:** This is how you see yourself in relation to others, shaped by the roles you play.

- **Family Roles:** Your identity within family dynamics, such as being a parent, sibling, or child.

- **Friendships and Social Networks:** How your social relationships influence your self-perception.

- **Romantic Relationships:** The impact of romantic partnerships on your identity.

- **Experiential Identity:** This is your individual experiences and the meaning you assign to them.

- **Life Experiences:** Events that significantly impact your life and shape your identity.

- **Narrative Identity:** The stories you tell yourself about your life, contributing to your self-concept.

- **Identity and Change:** Identity evolves through different life stages and transitions, adapting to changes.

- **Developmental Changes:** Shifts through life stages, from adolescence to adulthood.

- **Life Transitions:** Major changes like career shifts, relocations, or relationship changes.

- **Identity and Well-Being:** This facet explores the interplay between your identity and mental and emotional well-being.

- **Self-Compassion:** How kindly you treat yourself amid failures or difficulties.

- **Self-Efficacy:** Your belief in your ability to achieve goals and handle symptoms of an IDENTITY GAP.

Symptoms of an IDENTITY GAP

- **Behavioral Symptoms:** Inability to set or pursue meaningful goals, behavioral withdrawal, risk-taking behaviors, indecision, or changing interests.

- **Emotional Distress:** Feelings of confusion, anxiety, depression, low self-esteem, and diminished self-worth.

- **Physical Signs:** Fatigue, changing sleep patterns, and lack of energy.

- **Cognitive Symptoms:** Overthinking, identity confusion, and existential questions.

Embrace the Magic of Identity Transitions and Transformation

The IDENTITY GAP often emerges during significant life transitions. Closing the IDENTITY GAP is a journey of self-discovery and realignment. By recognizing the symptoms and understanding the drivers, you empower yourself to align your life more closely with your true self. Remember, your identity is like a gem—dynamic, evolving, and full of potential. Polish it with compassion, purpose, and vision. Illuminate your path with self-awareness and step confidently into the magic of your fullest potential.

Understanding these dimensions and their impact unlocks the secrets to closing your IDENTITY GAP and stepping into the most authentic, empowered version of yourself. You have the power to transform and align every facet of your identity with the life you truly desire. If you would like to explore further, please check out the "IDENTITY GAP Research" section at the end of this book.

Transitions—whether they involve a new career, a move to a different city, the end of a relationship, or a change in health—are natural parts of life. These moments often come with uncertainty and can create IDENTITY GAPs. However, they are also opportunities for growth, reinvention, and self-discovery.

Now that you've grasped the concept of the IDENTITY GAP, let's dive into how you can *Embrace Growth and Change* and why it is essential for unlocking your full potential to live a truly fulfilling life.

CHAPTER 3
EMBRACE GROWTH AND CHANGE

Imagine standing at the edge of a vast, unexplored cosmos. Behind you lies the safety of the known, the familiar routines that no longer inspire you. Before you, however, is a path filled with mystery, wonder, and the promise of transformation. Your heart beats faster, your hands tremble, and your mind begins to race with doubt. You hesitate, wondering if you should turn back, stay where it's safe, and avoid the risk of the unknown. But what if, instead of fearing what lies ahead, you chose to see this moment as the universe's call to adventure? What if, in the very act of stepping forward, you find not just your courage, but your true self? Who are you in this universe?

Change is life's most exhilarating challenge and greatest opportunity. It is not an obstacle, but an invitation to step into your highest potential. While the familiar feels safe, it's the uncharted territory that holds the real treasure. This is where growth happens. This is where you become the magician of your own life. Embrace change not as a disruption, but as a powerful force guiding you toward your true path. Yet, here's the truth: Change is not the enemy; it's the universe's way of nudging you toward your highest potential. It's the stars that sparkle like diamonds in the night sky, the eclipses, and the changing seasons, inviting you to step into your power and embrace a growth mindset.

Why Change Feels Challenging: Navigating the Dynamic Nature of Identity

Change—it's one of the few constants in life. Whether it's a new job, a shift in personal relationships, or a move to a new city, the landscape of our lives is always evolving. While change is inevitable, it can often feel daunting and overwhelming. The emotions that accompany change—fear, doubt, and anxiety—can seem like insurmountable obstacles. But here's the game-changer: your mindset.

A fixed mindset views change as a threat. It whispers, "you're not ready," "it's too risky," or "you might fail." Conversely, a growth mindset sees change as an ally. It recognizes that every shift, every challenge, every unexpected turn is an opportunity to grow, evolve, and transform. By adopting a growth mindset, you begin to see change not as a disruption but as an essential part of your journey—a gateway to new possibilities.

The Perils of Ignoring the Need for Change

In the classic book "Who Moved My Cheese?" by Spencer Johnson, the narrative centers around the struggles of characters who face significant changes in their lives. The story's message is clear: those who refuse to adapt to change will find themselves stuck, disoriented, and unfulfilled. The consequences of ignoring the need to pivot your identity are similar. When you cling to an outdated version of yourself or resist the urge to evolve, you may encounter several challenges:

- **Stagnation and Discontent:** Holding on to a static identity can lead to feelings of stagnation. You may feel like you are slowly sinking in quicksand, experience dissatisfaction, a sense of being unfulfilled, or a growing disconnect between who you are and who you want to be.

- **Missed Opportunities:** Failing to pivot your identity can cause you to overlook valuable opportunities for growth and success. New experiences and roles often come with the potential for personal and professional advancement. Ignoring these opportunities can limit your potential and keep you from achieving your goals.

- **Increased Stress and Anxiety:** When you resist change, you may find yourself battling internal resistance and stress. This can manifest as anxiety, frustration, and an overall sense of being overwhelmed. By embracing change, you can alleviate these feelings and cultivate a more balanced approach to life's transitions.

- **Lost Connection with Authentic Self:** If you hold tightly to an outdated identity, you risk losing touch with your true self. Your values, passions, and interests evolve over time, and failing to adapt means you may miss discovering and living in alignment with your authentic self.

How to Cultivate a Growth Mindset for Change

- **See Change as an Adventure, Not a Threat:** Embrace the idea that every change—whether big or small—is an adventure waiting to unfold. Instead of fearing the unknown, ask yourself, "What new experiences might this bring?" Reframe your perspective to focus on the excitement of discovery and growth. Growth often happens outside of your comfort zone, and viewing change as an adventure will help you unlock your limitless potential.

- **Become the Observer of Your Own Mind:** Pay attention to your thoughts when faced with change. Are they filled with fear or possibility? With a magician's touch, you can transform self-doubt into self-discovery. Whenever limiting beliefs surface— such as "I'm not ready" or "I'm not good enough"—challenge them. Replace these thoughts with affirmations like "I am capable," "I am evolving," and "I am open to new possibilities." Your mindset is a powerful tool; use it to your advantage.

- **Practice Resilience as Your Superpower:** Resilience is the ability to bounce back and adapt in the face of adversity. By embracing resilience, you step into your power as the magician of your own life. Approach challenges as opportunities to gain experience and grow. Ask yourself, "What can I learn from this? How can this experience shape me into the person I'm meant to become?" Each obstacle you overcome builds your strength and prepares you for future challenges.

- **Set Intentions, Not Limitations:** A fixed mindset sees only limitations, while a growth mindset sets powerful intentions. Shift from "I can't handle this change" to "I will grow through this change." Define your intentions and align your actions with these goals. Visualize the person you want to become, and let that vision guide your daily actions. Remind yourself of your intentions regularly and take steps— no matter how small—toward realizing them.

- **Celebrate Every Step of Your Transformation:** In your journey of change, acknowledge and celebrate every milestone, no matter how small. Each step forward, each moment of courage, and each lesson learned is a victory. Recognize and honor the growth occurring within you, even when progress feels slow or uncertain. Remember, transformation is not a destination but a continuous journey.

By embracing change, you step into the role of the magician, crafting your life with intention and purpose. Change is not a detour; it's the path that guides you toward self-actualization. It's your invitation to become who you are meant to be, to step into your magic, and to live a life that reflects the brilliance of your unique journey.

Deepening Your Growth Mindset: Embracing Change as a Magician of Your Own Life

Change can feel like standing on the edge of a cliff, peering into an unknown expanse. It's natural to feel fear, but what if you were to reframe that fear? Instead of worrying about falling, ask yourself, "What if I soar?" The essence of a growth mindset is about feeling fear and moving forward anyway.

- **The Power of Reframing: Turning Obstacles into Opportunities:** Reframing is a potent tool. When faced with change, view challenges from a different perspective. For example, if you're dealing with job loss or relocation, consider it a chance for reinvention. What new paths could this open for you? What skills or talents might you discover or develop? By reframing your perspective, you transform challenges into stepping stones for a richer, more authentic life.

- **Cultivating Self-Compassion: Your Secret Ingredient for Growth:** It's easy to be hard on yourself during times of change. Instead, offer yourself kindness and encouragement. Imagine speaking to yourself as you would to a dear friend facing similar challenges. Self-compassion allows you to navigate change with grace and patience, reminding you that growth is a journey, not a destination.

- **Harnessing the Power of Visualization: See the Life You Want to Create:** Visualization is a powerful tool. Picture the person you want to become and the life you want to lead. Envision yourself thriving in the face of change, handling challenges with confidence, and finding joy in new opportunities. The clearer your vision, the more your subconscious will work toward making it a reality.

- **Leveraging the Magic of Community: You Don't Have to Do It Alone:** You don't have to navigate change alone. Surround yourself with supportive individuals who inspire and challenge you. Whether it's a coach, mentor, friend, or support group, a community can provide valuable insights and encouragement. They remind you that you're not alone in your journey and can offer strength and courage in numbers.

- **Commit to Lifelong Learning: Growth is a Continuous Process:** A growth mindset thrives on learning. Seek out opportunities that challenge your thinking and expand your horizons. Reflect on what each experience teaches you about yourself and your values.

- **Trust in Your Inner Magician: You Are the Author of Your Own Story:** At the heart of embracing change with a growth mindset is trust. Trust in yourself, trust in the process, and trust in your journey. You are the author of your story. With each decision and action, you shape your narrative. Trust in your inner magician and embrace the unknown with confidence and curiosity.

Final Thoughts: Your Life, Your Magic, Your Masterpiece

Change is not a force to be feared but a powerful tool for growth. It's the universe's way of guiding you toward your true purpose and highest potential. Embrace change with an open heart, a growth mindset, and unwavering belief in yourself. You are the magician of your life—ready to create, transform, and manifest the extraordinary.

Embrace the incredible power of change and growth that resides within you. Trust in your ability to navigate transformation and witness how your life unfolds in extraordinary ways. Now, let's dive into the vital role of the grief process with *Shadow Dancer* and how it can be a profound part of your journey.

SHADOW DANCER

I was on a cross-town bus with no destination, drifting through the city like a ghost. The streets blurred into one another, and I found myself dancing in the shadows of self, lost in a haze of confusion and sorrow.

One evening, as twilight descended, I met a woman on one of those buses. She was unlike anyone I had ever encountered—her presence was both haunting and comforting. Her eyes held the depth of oceans, and when she spoke, it was as if the world itself hushed to listen.

"My name is Grief," she said, her voice soft but resonant, echoing through the chambers of my heart. I knew, in that moment, that she was my other half—my shadow. She was the embodiment of all I had lost, all the pain I had buried deep within.

Grief took my hand and led me off the bus, guiding me through the city until we arrived in a realm I had never seen before: the Land of Depth. Here, the sky was studded with diamonds, each one a crystallized truth, raining down like stars. Grief began to speak, her words weaving new dreams and spinning yarns of old stories. She whispered glimmers of truth, love, and grace, illuminating the path before me.

"Let me show you the wisdom hidden within your pain," she said, her voice a lullaby. In her embrace, I felt the weight of my sorrow lift, replaced by a profound sense of understanding. Grief revealed to me that every tear shed was a facet of a diamond, a piece of wisdom crystallized from the depths of my soul.

Together, we practiced a HeartMath Institute meditation, focusing on my breath and my heartbeat, aligning my mind with my heart. As I breathed in deeply, I imagined the diamonds in the sky descending into my chest, filling me with light, clarity, and my truth. The meditation guided me to a place of coherence, where my emotions and thoughts were in harmony, and I could hear Grief's voice more clearly than ever.

"Your pain is not your enemy," she whispered. "It is the source of your greatest wisdom and love."

In the Land of Depth, under the rain of diamonds, Grief helped me crystallize the truths I had long ignored, weaving them into a new story—one of resilience, grace, and a heart open to love and possibility.

CHAPTER 4
SHADOW DANCER

Grief: The Uninvited Companion on Your Journey

Grief is an uninvited companion that we all encounter at some point in our lives. It arrives unannounced, sometimes with devastating suddenness, other times with a slow, creeping inevitability. It can be triggered by any significant loss—whether it's the passing of a loved one, the end of a relationship, or the loss of a cherished dream. Grief is a profound, deeply personal process that can make us feel as though we are wandering through a dense fog, uncertain of when—or if—we will find clarity again.

But grief is more than just an emotional state; it is a multi-layered experience that affects the body, mind, and spirit. The American Psychological Association (APA) defines grief as the anguish experienced in response to a significant loss, often the death of a loved one, but it can also manifest in response to other losses, triggering physical symptoms like fatigue, sleep disturbances, and changes in appetite. It may show up as intense sadness, anger, confusion, or even numbness as we struggle to make sense of the loss and its impact on our lives.

Navigating the Process of Grief

Understanding the nature of grief can help you navigate through it. Elisabeth Kübler-Ross's five stages of grief–denial, anger, bargaining, depression, and acceptance—offer one way to comprehend this journey, but remember, grief is not a linear process. You may find yourself moving back and forth between these stages or experiencing them in a different order. Other models, like William Worden's Four Tasks of Mourning, provide additional frameworks for understanding grief. Worden's four tasks of mourning include accepting the reality of the loss, processing the pain of grief, adjusting to a world without what was lost, and finding a way to maintain a connection with the loss while moving forward.

While grief is a personal journey, here are steps that can guide you:

- Honor your emotions
- Seek support from your tribe
- Prioritize self-care
- Create sacred rituals
- Be compassionate with yourself

Grief, as painful as it is, can also be a doorway to transformation. By allowing yourself to grieve fully, seeking support, and taking intentional steps toward healing, you can emerge from the fog with renewed purpose and a deeper connection to your inner self and the world around you.

Grieving the Loss of Identity

Grief is not limited to losing loved ones or relationships; it also surfaces when we lose a part of our identity. You might grieve the loss of a career, a role, a dream, or a sense of who you thought you were. As a life coach, I've witnessed how grief weaves itself into every facet of our being—emotional, physical, cognitive, and spiritual. Understanding the symptoms of this unique form of grief is the key to navigating its complexities and finding a path forward.

Symptoms of Grief

1. **Emotional Symptoms:** Grief often feels like a heavy weight on your chest, making it hard to breathe or think clearly. You may feel sadness, despair, or even hopelessness. Emotions can swing wildly—one moment, tears flow freely; the next, you feel numb or detached. Guilt, regret, and anger may surface as you process your loss. It's vital to allow yourself to feel these emotions fully. Suppressing them will only prolong the healing process.

2. **Physical Symptoms:** Grief impacts the body. You may feel fatigued, have trouble sleeping, or notice changes in your appetite. Physical symptoms like headaches, muscle tension, or chest pain are common. Your immune system may weaken, making you more susceptible to illness.

3. **Cognitive Symptoms:** Grieving your identity often brings confusion and forgetfulness. You might replay past events, second-guess your decisions, or question your sense of self. Overthinking becomes a constant companion, often accompanied by a relentless inner critic. Concentration, decision-making, and presence may feel impaired. These disruptions are your brain's way of trying to make sense of your new reality.

4. **Behavioral Symptoms:** Grief can change your behavior in subtle and surprising ways. You might withdraw from social activities, become irritable or restless, or engage in risky behaviors like substance abuse. You may find comfort in repetitive actions or habits, offering a temporary sense of control amid emotional chaos. Recognizing these behaviors is essential to understanding whether they help or hinder your healing.

5. **Spiritual Symptoms:** Grieving your identity can shake your spiritual foundations. You might question your beliefs or feel anger toward a higher power. Conversely, you might seek solace in spiritual practices that help you find meaning in your suffering. This period of spiritual questioning can

lead to profound growth as you search for answers in a new context.

Grief as a Normal Part of Life and Career Transitions

Grief is not an anomaly but a normal and natural response to many kinds of losses throughout our lives—including those we experience in our careers and identities. When you face a significant change, such as transitioning careers, retiring, moving to a new city, or redefining your sense of purpose, grief can emerge as a companion on your journey.

Grief during life and career transitions appears because something has ended, and something new is beginning. Even if the change is desired, there is often a sense of loss for what was left behind—whether it's a familiar routine, a sense of competence, or the predictability of your old life. These losses can trigger feelings of sadness, confusion, or fear as you face the unknown.

Grief can also arise from a perceived loss of identity. If you have always identified yourself by your job title, role, or a specific aspect of your life, a significant change can feel like losing a part of who you are. This sense of identity loss can create deep, existential grief as you work to redefine yourself and find new meaning.

Embracing Grief as an Opportunity for Transformation

Grief is often uncomfortable, but it is also a powerful teacher. It offers an opportunity to reflect on what truly matters, what you want to carry forward, and what you are ready to release. It invites you to confront parts of your identity that may be tied to outdated beliefs or external expectations.

By embracing grief as a natural part of your journey, you transform it from something to be feared into a source of strength and clarity. Allow yourself to mourn what was lost, but remain open to new possibilities. Remember, grief is not a sign of weakness; it is a testament to your capacity to grow, adapt, and evolve.

Grief is a sign that you are living fully, embracing change, and stepping into new possibilities. The feelings you experience reflect the depth of your journey and the courage it takes to redefine who you are. By understanding that grief is a normal part of life's transitions, you allow yourself the grace to feel, heal, and transform. As we stand at the crossroads of identity, there is an inevitable mourning for the person we once were. Whether shaped by careers, relationships, or life's unpredictable currents, the loss of an identity can feel like a deep, personal death. We grieve for the version of ourselves that no longer fits, as if shedding a second skin. This grief is necessary—a dance in the shadows—where we wrestle with ghosts of the past, the dreams that went unrealized, and the masks we've outgrown.

In these moments, the shadows whisper truths we may have tried to ignore: the fear of stepping into the unknown, the guilt for outgrowing old roles, the anger at the unfairness of change. We often seek comfort in the familiar, but the time comes when the dance must end. Our steps, once tentative in the dark, must find rhythm again in the light of a new beginning.

It's here, at the edge of mourning, where we have a choice—to stay lost in the shadowlands or to rise, ready to reclaim and rebuild what has been broken. Every identity lost leaves a vault, a sacred space, waiting to be filled with new stories, new roles, and new definitions of self.

As we turn the page to the next chapter, **The Identity Vault**, know that this is the place where we begin the work of reconstruction. It's time to unlock the vault of your true self. Here, we won't bury the past but rather honor it as a foundation. We will rebuild—facet by facet—an identity that's not bound by old definitions but enriched by them. This is the transformation, the crystallization of your new self. Let's begin the next step: rebuilding your identity.

CHAPTER 5
THE IDENTITY VAULT

The Identity Vault: Unlocking Your Dreams Before It's Too Late

The number one regret people have in life is that they didn't live the life of their dreams. But how can you chase the right dream when you're stuck in an IDENTITY GAP? It's impossible to pursue the future you desire if you're not aligned with who you truly are.

Research shows that most college students choose the wrong career path. By the time they reach mid-career, many feel trapped in a degree and job they no longer identify with—burdened by student loan debt, credit card bills, mortgages, and family responsibilities. They feel stuck, stressed, and unsure of how to make a change. Do you celebrate Friday only to have dread set in by Sunday when you think about returning to work? Burnout rates are skyrocketing, and anxiety and depression are common among professionals who feel their work is misaligned with their identity.

Think about this: you spend one-third of your life at work. If your job doesn't align with your true self, it will affect the other areas of your life. That one-third of your life spent sleeping may be disrupted and plagued by stress or insomnia. And what about the final one-third of your life—the time that's supposed to be yours? It suffers, too.

But what if you could change that? What if you could rewrite your life and start living the dream you've always wanted? It begins by closing the IDENTITY GAP and realigning who you are with what you do. Most people don't have the tools to make informed decisions about their careers and life path, and that's where it all begins. In the world of design, it's about asking the right questions to find solutions. These questions can help you pivot, avoid burnout, and avoid that ultimate regret—that you never lived the life of your dreams.

Let's begin building your identity compass—a guide that helps you crystallize your purpose, path, and pivot points. When you stay in a job that doesn't reflect your true self, you risk burning out and losing your professional identity. What would you lose if you burned out completely?

In this chapter, we'll work to align that 55% of your identity with the other dimensions of wellness. When your career and life are in harmony, you'll experience more energy, happiness, and freedom to pursue your passions.

Of course, no single book can give you every tool you need, or it would feel like a manual, and you wouldn't read it. That's why this is just the beginning. Visit elysiandream.net for coaching, courses, and tools designed to help you assess and close your IDENTITY GAP. Now, let's design the life of your dreams. It's time to unlock The Identity Vault.

The Psychological Impact of the IDENTITY GAP: How to Align Your Life for True Fulfillment

Are you feeling adrift, questioning your path, and sensing that something is missing in your life? The IDENTITY GAP might be the hidden force behind this inner conflict. When your true self is out of alignment with the roles you play, it can feel like being lost in space with no clear exit. But what if closing this gap could lead you to a life filled with purpose, joy, and eudaimonia (Greek)—the thriving state of being your best self? Let's explore how intentional goal setting, self-reflection, and redefining success can help you bridge this gap and live a more fulfilling life.

The Dynamic Nature of Identity

Let's clear something up—identity isn't static. It's not a box you check once and move on from; it's a dynamic, ever-evolving part of who you are. As you grow, your identity grows with you. It shifts and changes with your experiences, relationships, and the stages of life you move through. Look back at who you were five, ten, or even twenty years ago. You're not the same person, and that's a good thing!

But if you're holding on tightly to an outdated version of yourself, you might feel stuck, anxious, or even a bit lost. You've always identified as a "successful corporate executive," but deep down, you're yearning for a more creative or entrepreneurial path. Or you've been seen as the "reliable caregiver" for so long that you've lost touch with your adventurous side.

Recognizing that your identity is fluid and flexible is empowering. It gives you the freedom to explore new facets of yourself, embrace change, and evolve into a version of yourself that feels more authentic and fulfilling. When you open yourself up to this dynamic process, you give yourself permission to grow and thrive.

The Magic of Knowing Yourself

There's nothing more powerful than truly knowing who you are. It allows you to live with purpose, passion, and authenticity. As you explore the dimensions of your identity, remember that you are a unique, ever-evolving individual—capable of remarkable things. Your identity is like a gemstone; it shines brighter when polished with self-awareness, self-compassion, and self-love.

Start today. Dive deep into who you are, embrace the changes, and take bold steps toward closing any IDENTITY GAPs. You have the power to transform your life and step into your fullest, most authentic self. Your journey to self-discovery is not just about finding yourself—it's about creating the person you were always meant to be.

What Happens When You Don't Pivot Your Identity

Failing to pivot your identity can lead to stagnation and frustration. It may prevent you from seizing new opportunities, hinder your personal growth, and exacerbate feelings of dissatisfaction. By embracing the dynamic nature of your identity, you unlock the potential to live a more fulfilling, authentic life. So, dive deep into who you are, embrace change, and take bold steps toward closing any IDENTITY GAPs. You have the power to transform your life and step into your fullest, most authentic self. Your journey of self-discovery is about creating the person you were always meant to be.

When you don't pivot your identity in response to new experiences and growth opportunities, you risk falling into several pitfalls:

- **Feeling Stuck:** Clinging to an outdated identity can make you feel trapped in a life that no longer fits. It's like trying to wear clothes that don't match your current style or size. You might find yourself going through the motions but without genuine fulfillment.

- **Missed Opportunities:** If you're not open to evolving, you might miss exciting new opportunities that could bring joy and growth. Embracing change often leads to discovering new passions, skills, and aspects of yourself that you never knew existed.

- **Increased Anxiety:** Holding onto a static identity can create anxiety, especially when external circumstances change. You may feel a heightened sense of discomfort or stress because your identity doesn't align with your current reality.

- **Diminished Self-Worth:** When you're not in tune with who you are becoming, your sense of self-worth may suffer. You might feel inadequate or disconnected because your identity is misaligned with your evolving desires and aspirations.

The IDENTITY GAP and Its Psychological Effects

The IDENTITY GAP—the space between who you are and who you want to be—can create a profound sense of psychological stress. You might feel lost, uncertain, and anxious, struggling to find direction. This gap often triggers a crisis of identity, where your values, beliefs, and purpose come into question. The familiar roles that once brought meaning and structure now feel misaligned, leaving a void that's challenging to fill.

This sense of disorientation can lead to feelings of inadequacy, imposter syndrome, and fear of failure. The pressure to quickly adapt to new roles or expectations without sufficient time for self-reflection often results in emotional exhaustion. To move forward, it's crucial to understand the underlying forces that shape this gap.

External Pressures: Social Expectations and Their Impact

Social expectations, family demands, and workplace norms can amplify the IDENTITY GAP. Society frequently imposes rigid timelines and success metrics, urging us to conform to identities that may not resonate with our authentic selves. For instance, you might feel compelled to pursue a high-status career despite a deep desire for a more meaningful but less prestigious path. This inner conflict can widen the gap, leading to increased stress and self-doubt.

Moreover, our social roles are deeply ingrained, making it hard to break free from the identities that have defined us for years. A stay-at-home parent returning to the workforce, for example, may struggle to reconcile their nurturing role with the demands of a competitive professional environment. Aligning your identity with your true self requires intention, reflection, and sometimes the courage to challenge societal norms.

Closing the IDENTITY GAP: Strategies for Intentional Growth

Bridging the IDENTITY GAP is not a passive process; it requires conscious effort, goal setting, and self-reflection. Here are strategies to help you navigate this journey:

- **Seek Support**: Surround yourself with people who support your journey. Mentors, coaches, or therapists can provide guidance and insights as you navigate this period of transition. They can help you explore new possibilities, set meaningful goals, and offer encouragement when doubts arise.

- **Step Outside Your Comfort Zone:** Engage in new experiences, meet new people, or try activities you've never attempted before. Expanding your horizons can help you discover new facets of who you are and what you're capable of.

- **Self-Reflection and Awareness:** Begin by reflecting on your past identities and how they have shaped your current self-concept. Consider how these identities served you at different life stages and how they may need to evolve to align with your current goals and values. Write down your thoughts to gain clarity. Be available for regular self-reflection. Journaling, meditating, or simply spending quiet time with your thoughts can help you tune in to what's really going on inside. Ask yourself questions like, "What truly makes me happy?" or "What do I stand for?" The answers will help reveal your core identity.

The Journey to Eudaimonia: Aligning Your Identity

When you intentionally bridge the IDENTITY GAP, you are aligning your life with your true self, which can lead to a state of **eudaimonia**—a profound sense of happiness and fulfillment that arises from living in accordance with your values, purpose, and potential. This alignment is not just about achieving external goals but also about cultivating an inner harmony that resonates with who you truly are.

The following are steps to help you on this journey:

1. **Define Your Core Values:** Identify what matters most to you. Your values are the bedrock of your identity. What principles guide your decisions? Understanding your core values will help you align your life with what truly resonates with you.

Values Clarification Exercise:

Your core values are the foundation of your identity. When your life choices align with your values, you feel fulfilled and authentic. When they don't, an IDENTITY GAP emerges.

- Reflect on what truly matters to you. What principles guide your decisions? Write down the top five values that are most important to you.

- Evaluate your current life: Are your daily actions and decisions aligned with these values? If not, where is the disconnect?

- For each value that doesn't align with your current life, consider what changes you would need to make to better reflect this value.

2. **Know Your Strengths:** Working in a job that leverages your strengths allows you to thrive, boosting both your performance and satisfaction. When your role aligns with what you naturally excel at, you feel more engaged, confident, and fulfilled in your work. When you are not aligned with your strengths, it can feel like you are fighting an uphill battle.

3. **Dive Into Your Passions and Interests:** What activities make you feel alive? What pursuits make you lose track of time? Your passions are powerful indicators of your authen-

tic self. Embrace them and find ways to weave them into your daily routine.

4. **Examine Your Roles:** Consider the various roles you play—parent, partner, leader, and friend. How do these roles shape your identity? Are there roles that no longer fit or new ones you wish to explore? Reflecting on this can help align your life with your evolving self.

5. **Examine Your Habits:** Habits play a crucial role in shaping our identity, as they are the consistent actions that define who we are and who we become. According to James Clear, author of *Atomic Habits*, "Every action you take is a vote for the type of person you wish to become" (Clear, 2018). By cultivating habits aligned with our desired self-image, we reinforce and solidify our personal and professional identity over time.

6. **Goal Setting with Intention:** Identify what truly matters to you and set goals that reflect those values. Align your actions with these goals to create a life that feels meaningful and fulfilling. Set clear, achievable goals that align with your true self. Think about what you want to achieve, both personally and professionally, and create a roadmap to get there. Be specific about the steps you will take and set a timeline to stay on track. As you align your actions with your values, you'll experience greater satisfaction, reduced anxiety, and a deeper sense of purpose.

7. **Redefine Success:** Challenge the conventional definitions of success that have been imposed on you. What does success truly mean for you? Is it about prestige, wealth, or something deeper, like happiness, connection, or purpose? Define success on your own terms and create a life that aligns with this vision.

8. **Future Self Visualization:** Close your eyes and imagine your ideal life five years from now. What does it look like? What are you doing, and who are you with? Write down a detailed description of this future self, including specifics about your career, relationships, lifestyle, and achievements.

Compare this vision with your current life to identify gaps. Reflect on what's holding you back and what steps you can take to bridge these gaps.

9. **Integrate Past and Present:** Work towards integrating your past experiences and identities with your current aspirations. This integration creates a more cohesive and resilient sense of self, helping you navigate future transitions with confidence. Reflect on how each experience, both positive and negative, has contributed to your growth.

10. **Practice Mindfulness and Build Resilience:** Engage in mindfulness practices to stay grounded during uncertain times. Meditation, journaling, and deep breathing can help you remain present and centered. Build resilience by setting healthy boundaries, practicing self-care, and maintaining a positive outlook, even when facing challenges.

11. **Practice Self-Compassion:** Be gentle with yourself during times of change. It's normal to feel lost or uncertain. Show yourself the same kindness and understanding you would offer a friend in a comparable situation.

As we work to close the IDENTITY GAP, one crucial step remains: aligning who you truly are with the core domains of wellness. Your well-being depends on it—because without that harmony, you'll always feel a disconnect. So now, let's take the plunge into what truly sustains you. Let's dive into wellness—where your life and identity can finally meet.

The 8 Domains of Wellness: Aligning Life and Career for Optimal Living

Imagine living a life where every dimension of your being is in harmony, like the facets of a perfectly cut diamond, each reflecting its own brilliance while contributing to a magnificent whole. That's the magic of aligning your life and career with the eight domains of wellness. By consciously integrating these areas, you can unlock a life filled with purpose, energy, and fulfillment.

I remember working in a clinic where many patients were heavily medicated. After listening to their stories, a common theme emerged: they felt stuck in their lives and careers and didn't know how to pivot toward work that aligned with their purpose. They were disconnected from themselves, unable to see the path forward.

1. **Emotional Wellness: Mastering Your Inner World**

   Embrace your emotional landscape as a powerful source of insight and guidance. Emotional wellness is not just about feeling good; it's about understanding and navigating your emotions with wisdom. Develop emotional intelligence, practice self-compassion, and learn to transform challenges into opportunities for growth. When your emotions are aligned, your decisions are guided by intuition, clarity, and confidence.

- **How do you currently feel about your emotional well-being?** Are there specific emotions or patterns that you notice frequently?

- **In what areas of your life do you feel emotionally out of balance?** What impact does this imbalance have on your daily life?

- **How do you express or process your emotions?** Do you have healthy outlets or methods for managing your emotions?

- **What situations or people tend to drain your emotional energy?** How do you currently protect or restore your emotional energy?

- **How aligned are your daily habits and relationships with your emotional needs?** Are there any adjustments you feel you need to make to improve your emotional wellness?

- **What role does self-compassion play in your emotional well-being?** How do you treat yourself during emotionally challenging times?

- **What brings you emotional fulfillment, and how often do you engage in those activities?** Are you prioritizing the things that bring you joy and emotional balance?

2. **Physical Wellness: Energizing Your Life Force**

    Your body is the vessel through which you experience life's magic. Physical wellness is more than exercise and nutrition; it's about nurturing your body's innate vitality. Prioritize restorative sleep, mindful movement, and nourishing foods that fuel your body and mind. When your physical wellness is optimized, you have the energy to pursue your dreams and create the life you desire. About 5% of your identity comes from your physical attributes and health.

- **How do you feel about your physical health and energy levels?** Are there any specific concerns or patterns you've noticed?

- **What daily habits support your physical well-being?** Are there any habits you feel are hindering your health?

- **How do you currently approach nutrition and exercise?** Are these areas aligned with your physical wellness goals?

- **How does your body respond to stress, and how do you manage it physically?** Are there techniques you use to alleviate physical tension or fatigue?

- **Are you getting enough rest and recovery?** How aligned is your sleep quality with your overall physical needs?

- **What are the signals your body gives when it's feeling imbalanced or unhealthy?** How do you respond to those signals?

- **How do your work and lifestyle affect your physical wellness?** Are there adjustments you can make to better support your body's needs?

3. **Intellectual Wellness: Expanding Your Horizons**

Feed your mind with curiosity, knowledge, and creativity. Intellectual wellness is about embracing a lifelong love of learning and keeping your mind sharp and adaptable. Engage in activities that challenge your thinking, spark creativity, and encourage you to see the world from new perspectives. When you expand your intellectual boundaries, you cultivate a mindset that's open to new possibilities and innovative solutions.

- **How do you challenge yourself to grow intellectually?** Are there activities or practices that stimulate your mind regularly?

- **What new skills or knowledge are you currently developing?** How do these align with your personal or professional goals?

- **How do you stay curious and open to new ideas?** Are there areas of your life where you feel intellectually stagnant?

- **What role does creativity or problem-solving play in your daily life?** How can you incorporate more of these into your routine?

- **How do you engage with others in meaningful, thought-provoking conversations?** Are there opportunities for you to connect with like-minded individuals or explore new perspectives?

- **How do you manage information overload or mental fatigue?** What boundaries do you set to protect your intellectual wellness?

- **How does your current work or personal life support your intellectual growth?** Are there areas where you could seek more intellectual stimulation or learning opportunities?

4. Social Wellness: Building Meaningful Connections

We are wired for connection, and social wellness is about cultivating a support network that nourishes your soul. Choose relationships that inspire growth, kindness, and authenticity. Be the magician who creates spaces where others feel seen, heard, and valued. When your social life aligns with your values, it becomes a source of joy, belonging, and mutual empowerment. About 20% of your identity comes from your personal relationships, and 10% comes from your background and culture, which has influence over your relationships.

- **How satisfied are you with the quality of your relationships?** Are there key relationships in your life that need attention or improvement?

- **Do you feel a sense of belonging within your social circles or community?** Where do you feel most connected, and where do you feel disconnected?

  How do you nurture and maintain your social connections? Are there people in your life you wish to reconnect with or deepen your relationship with?

- **How comfortable are you in setting boundaries with others?** Are you able to balance social obligations with your personal needs?

- **What role does support from others play in your well-being?** How do you seek or offer support in your relationships?

- **How do you handle conflicts or challenges in your social interactions?** Are there any unresolved social tensions that need addressing?

- **How do you engage in activities that foster a sense of community?** Are there groups or networks that align with your values and interests?

5. **Spiritual Wellness: Aligning with Your Higher Purpose**

Step into the realm of spiritual wellness by exploring the deeper meaning of your existence. This domain is not confined to religion—it's about connecting with your inner essence, finding purpose, and living in alignment with your core values. Meditate, reflect, and practice gratitude to tap into a profound sense of peace and direction. When you are spiritually aligned, every step you take is guided by a purpose greater than yourself.

- **What practices or rituals help you feel connected to something greater than yourself?** How regularly do you engage in these practices?

- **How do you define your sense of purpose or meaning in life?** What experiences have shaped your understanding of this purpose?

- **In what ways do you nurture your inner self or spirituality?** Are there activities that help you feel grounded or fulfilled?

- **How do you handle moments of doubt or disconnection in your spiritual journey?** What strategies do you use to reconnect when you feel lost?

- **What beliefs or values are most important to you?** How do these beliefs influence your daily life and decisions?

- **How do you find peace and acceptance in challenging times?** Are there specific practices that help you cultivate resilience?

- **What role does community or fellowship play in your spiritual life?** Do you seek out like-minded individuals for support and connection?

6. **Occupational Wellness: Crafting Your Dream Career**

Occupational wellness is about aligning your career with your passions, talents, and values. It's not just about what you do, but how you do it. Find meaning in your work, pursue opportunities for growth, and create a balance that allows you to enjoy both professional success and personal satisfaction. When your career aligns with who you truly are, work becomes a powerful expression of your authentic self.

As mentioned earlier, about 55% of your identity comes from your occupation. That's right—over half of who you are is tied to the work you do. What you spend your time doing shapes your identity. So, how do you design not just a job, but a lifestyle that aligns with all dimensions of your wellness? A lifestyle that fuels your passion and purpose rather than drains your energy. Is the one-third of your life that you spend working affecting the one-third of your life that you spend sleeping? Consider how that two-thirds of your life is impacting the rest of your dimensions of wellness. Is your career your whole identity?

- Are you one of the 99% of students who choose the wrong degree?

- Are you one of the 40% of college graduates who have regrets?

- Are you one of the 47% of mid-career professionals who feel you made the wrong career choice?

- Have you revised your values to accommodate your career?

- Are you one of the 20% who enjoys the work you do every day?

- Are you part of the 50% of the workforce who lack purpose and meaning?

- Is your work congruent with who you are?

- Do you feel fulfilled in your path?

- Do you know what your life purpose is?

- Is your career aligned with long-term goals and values?

- Does your career fit with your interests and passions?

- Are you motivated and energized by your career?

- Do you feel drained and exhausted by the work that you do?

- Are you working in a job that pays well but leaves you miserable?

- Do you want to pivot to a new career, feel stuck by debt and obligations, or fear starting over?

- Are you stuck beneath the glass ceiling or, worse, standing on a glass cliff—poised to fail?

- Are you pursuing a career to fulfill someone else's dream instead of your own?

- Are you one of the 89% in burnout?

- Do you have a work-life balance in your current position?

- What workplace stressors are you experiencing?

- Are there opportunities for advancement and growth?

- Are you in a transition: college-bound student, mid-career professional seeking change, midlife career struggles, retiree, or transitioning from the military?

- Do you feel appreciated and valued at work?

- Is your workplace culture negatively affecting you?

- Are you stuck in the pay gap?

- How are you managing work and life stress?

- Are you taking prescription medications to manage stress or depression caused by your job?

7. **Environmental Wellness: Creating Your Sanctuary**

Your environment shapes your energy, mood, and productivity. Environmental wellness involves creating spaces that inspire and rejuvenate you, whether it's your home, workplace, or natural surroundings. Keep your environment clean, organized, and filled with elements that bring you joy and peace. When your surroundings reflect your values and aspirations, you create a sanctuary that supports your journey.

- **How does your current environment (home, workplace, community) affect your overall well-being?** Are there aspects that enhance or detract from your wellness?

- **What steps do you take to create a space that feels nurturing and supportive?** How do you incorporate nature or elements that bring you peace?

- **In what ways do you practice sustainability in your daily life?** What small changes have you made to reduce your environmental impact?

- **How do you feel about the amount of time you spend outdoors?** What activities do you enjoy that connects you to nature?

- **What values do you hold regarding the health of the planet?** How do these values influence your lifestyle choices?

- **How do you respond to environmental stressors, such as noise or pollution?** What strategies do you use to mitigate their effects on your well-being?

- **What actions can you take to foster a sense of community in your environment?** How might these actions contribute to both your wellness and the well-being of others?

8. **Financial Wellness: Empowering Your Future**

   Financial wellness is about more than just money; it's about freedom, security, and the power to create the life you want. Develop a healthy relationship with money by understanding your financial goals, managing resources wisely, and aligning your spending with your values. When you master financial wellness, you are free to invest in your dreams, support causes that matter and live with abundance.

- **How do you feel about your current financial situation?** What emotions come up when you think about your finances?

- **What are your short-term and long-term financial goals?** How clear are you on the steps needed to achieve them?

- **What beliefs do you hold about money that may influence your financial decisions?** Are there any limiting beliefs you'd like to change?

- **How do you prioritize your spending in relation to your values and goals?** What areas of your budget feel aligned or misaligned with your priorities?

- **What strategies do you currently use to save and invest?** Are there any changes you feel ready to make in this area?

- **How do you handle financial stress or unexpected expenses?** What coping mechanisms or support systems do you have in place?

- **What steps can you take to increase your financial literacy and confidence?** Are there resources or tools you'd like to explore further?

- **Do you feel trapped in your job because the pay is good?** Consider how this may impact the other dimensions of your wellness.

Aligning the Domains for a Magically Balanced Life

Other facets of your identity to factor in are that 10% of your identity comes from personal values and beliefs and 5% from your hobbies, with variable percentages in gender, sexuality, life experiences, and personal history. Each of these domains is like a piece of a puzzle; when they fit together, they create a picture of a life fully lived. Aligning your life and career with these eight domains of wellness is the key to optimizing your existence, transforming each day into a magical adventure where you are the hero, the creator, and the architect of your destiny. Remember, you are not just living a life; you are crafting a masterpiece.

Step boldly into this journey, wield your magic wisely, and align every facet of your being for a life that sparkles with potential and purpose.

Crystallized Confidence

Crystallized confidence is a powerful state of being akin to the resilience of a diamond. Just as diamonds form under immense pressure, our confidence is forged through experiences that challenge us, shaping our character and fortitude. Embracing the notion of "failing forward" allows us to view setbacks not as failures, but as stepping stones toward growth. Each misstep becomes a valuable lesson, teaching us about our capabilities and potential.

Like the multifaceted nature of a diamond, confidence is not one-dimensional. It encompasses various aspects of our identity—our skills, values, and passions. By acknowledging and celebrating these facets, we can cultivate a deeper sense of self-worth. This multidimensional confidence empowers us to take risks, pursue our dreams, and face life's uncertainties with unwavering resolve.

When we recognize the power within ourselves, we tap into an unbreakable spirit. This inner strength fuels our ability to overcome obstacles and rise above challenges, reminding us that we are capable of more than we often realize. As we navigate the complexities of life, let us remember that, like diamonds, we shine brightest when polished by experience. By embracing our journey and crystallizing our confidence, we not only transform our self-perception but also inspire others to see the beauty and strength that resides within them. Embrace your inner diamond; the world is waiting for your brilliance to shine.

Aligning for a More Fulfilling Life

Recognizing and addressing your IDENTITY GAP is the first step toward living a more authentic and fulfilling life. By understanding where your self-concept and self-ideal diverge, you can begin the process of realignment. Remember, your identity is fluid and evolving; the goal is not to achieve perfect alignment but to continually strive toward a more authentic expression of who you are and who you want to become.

As you work through these exercises and reflect on your journey, keep in mind that this process is about rediscovering the self that has always been there waiting to be understood, embraced, and celebrated. This content incorporates actionable strategies that empower the reader to take control of their professional identity development.

Now that you've gained insight into developing and pivoting your identity, it's time to take the next step and explore the in-between spaces of *Liminal Thinking*.

CHAPTER 6
LIMINAL THINKING

Liminal Thinking: Crystallizing Identity in the Gap

IMAGINE THIS: You are standing at the edge of a dream, caught in the stillness between who you were and who you are becoming. It's a moment of both uncertainty and potential—a liminal space where all the facets of your being begin to crystallize like a diamond under pressure.

This is **the IDENTITY GAP**, the space between your past and future selves, where your true essence can emerge if you embrace it with the right mindset. We often feel lost in this gap, like wandering through a dreamscape where nothing feels fully formed. But the magician's power lies in the ability to see beyond the chaos and confusion, to **recognize that this gap is where transformation happens**. The space where you can be present and get into the flow of the experience so you can create your next chapter.

Liminal thinking is the process of embracing this in-between space, allowing it to shape and refine you. Rather than resisting uncertainty, you dive into it, trusting that the rough edges of your identity will polish into something brilliant—just like a diamond. This gap is where you can shed old layers and crystallize who you truly are.

Think of a diamond: it begins as carbon, a raw and unformed element until it undergoes immense pressure and heat. Only then does it emerge as one of the hardest, most beautiful materials on Earth. Your identity is no different. In the liminal space, all the facets of who you are—your dreams, your experiences, your values—come together to form a whole. This isn't about striving for perfection, but about acknowledging your shadows and embracing the *occlusions*—the unique imperfections that shape your character like a diamond. Consider it this way: no one is captivated by stories with flawless characters; it's their complexity and flaws that make them interesting and relatable. In liminal thinking, you are not the victim of circumstances—you are the architect of your identity. You are the dreamer looking past the veil of confusion, crafting your future with every choice you make. Every experience, every challenge is a tool in your alchemist's kit, shaping the facets of your diamond-like self. The **IDENTITY GAP** may feel overwhelming, but **it's where the magic of self-discovery unfolds**.

As you journey through the gap, ask yourself: What parts of me are ready to be crystallized? What facets of my identity are waiting to shine? What dreams am I prepared to bring into reality? **Liminal thinking empowers you to embrace the mystery,** to dream big, and to transform the chaos into clarity. This gap isn't a void—it's a powerful space of creation, where you can **crystallize the truest version of yourself and emerge like a diamond, resilient, multifaceted, and unbreakable.**

So, are you ready to explore the unknown and craft your future with intention? Your next chapter awaits, and the magic is already within you, waiting to be unleashed.

Journal Exercise 1: Exploring the Gap

Take a moment to journal about a current transition or challenge you are facing. Write down how you feel about being in the "in-between" space—neither where you were nor where you want to be. Then, ask yourself:

▪ What aspects of my identity are shifting in this gap?

- What am I resisting? What am I ready to release?

- How can I be more open and curious about this transition?

The magician archetype invites you to harness the energy of this gap, to see beyond the veil of confusion, and to step into your true power. Like a spell cast over time, each experience in the gap is an opportunity to gain experience, grow, and evolve. The secret to navigating this space is embracing curiosity, trusting the process, and knowing that the unknown is not your enemy but your greatest ally.

In liminal thinking, you are not the victim of circumstances— you are the architect of your identity. You are the dreamer, crafting your future with every choice you make. Every experience and challenge is a tool in your alchemist's kit, shaping the facets of your diamond-like self. The **IDENTITY GAP** may feel overwhelming, but **it's where the magic of self-discovery unfolds**.

Journal Exercise 2: Crystallizing Your Identity

To crystallize your identity, you need to align all the facets of your life. Write down the key areas of your life (career, relationships, health, spirituality, etc.). Reflect on each area and ask:

- What facet of myself needs the most attention or transformation?

- Which part of me feels fully aligned, and where am I out of alignment?

- What would it feel like to integrate all these facets into a unified, crystalline self?

Liminal thinking empowers you to embrace the mystery, to dream big, and to transform the chaos into clarity. This gap isn't a void—it's a powerful space of creation where you can **crystallize the truest version of yourself and emerge like a diamond-resilient, multifaceted, and unbreakable.**

Journal Exercise 3: The Power of Your Name in Shaping Identity

What's in a name? More than you might think. Your name is your *personal magic*, a symbol of your identity, power, and potential. From the moment it's given to you, it shapes how the world sees you—and how you see yourself. It's the first spell cast in the journey of becoming *who you truly are*.

Your name holds a key to your essence. It may carry the legacy of your ancestors, the dreams of your family, or the hope for who you might become. Over time, you *crystallize* your own meaning into it, like *shaping a diamond* through the experiences of your life. How does your name make you feel when you say it? Does it reflect your *true self* or an identity waiting to be unlocked?

The *power of your name* lies in how you choose to wear it, embrace its meaning, or *reshape it in your image*. In the end, *your name is a talisman*—a symbol of your *transformation* and journey toward wholeness. As you step deeper into the adventure of *self-discovery*, remember that your name is the gateway to your story, a doorway into *your true potential* and the unfolding of your unique *magic*.

What is the *energy* behind your name? Does it reflect your purpose? Knowing this helps you align with who you're destined to become.

Worldbuilding Your Identity: Crystallizing Who You Are in the Liminal Dreamscape

Worldbuilding isn't just a tool for writers and creators—it's a powerful way to envision and construct your own identity, especially when you find yourself navigating life's liminal phases, caught between the known and the unknown, the familiar and the new. When your sense of self feels fragmented, like a rocket breaking apart post-launch, worldbuilding can provide the framework to help you safely launch your dreams to crystallize your identity and its facets, like a dreamscape of your own making. Think of your identity as a world you are constantly building and refining. Like in any epic story, you are the protagonist, but you are also the architect, shaping the terrain, the rules, and the overarching narrative that will guide you. Your journey through chaos, uncertainty, or change can feel overwhelming, but these moments are crucial for discovering the raw materials that define who you are.

Mapping the Terrain: Your Core Values and Beliefs

The foundation of your world is built on your core values and beliefs. Take time to map out what truly matters to you. Just as an author develops the geography of a fictional world, identify the values that form your personal landscape. Are they rooted in family, creativity, growth, and freedom? These become the unshakable mountains and rivers that guide you through the liminal dreamscape.

Characters: Your Facets and Archetypes:

Like any rich world, your identity consists of multiple characters or facets, which represent various aspects of who you are. You are part Hero, facing challenges head-on, and part Magician, transforming obstacles into opportunities. As you build these facets into your personal narrative, you crystallize the diverse parts of your identity into something whole and resilient, just like the facets of a diamond.

Creating the Rules: Boundaries and Empowerment

In any well-constructed world, rules govern how things operate. For your world, these are the boundaries you set for yourself and others. Boundaries help define the space in which your identity can safely grow, free from external pressure or chaos. What are the non-negotiables for your self-care, your dreams, and your emotional health? Establish these "rules" to protect your energy and allow your identity to crystallize without interference.

Navigating the Chaos: Embracing Liminal Spaces

Liminal spaces—those in-between places where transformation happens—are often seen as chaotic and unsettling. But in worldbuilding, chaos is where creation begins. Embrace the chaos not as something to escape but as a fertile ground for discovery. In these moments of uncertainty, you can experiment, reimagine, and reconstruct who you are. Just as worlds evolve in stories, your identity grows and crystallizes through exploration and trial.

The Dreamscape: Visioning Your Future Self

In the dreamscape of your identity, anything is possible. Use visioning exercises to imagine your future self on the other side of chaos and liminality. What does your world look like once your identity has fully crystallized? What dreams are you pursuing? Who are you becoming? By vividly imagining this version of yourself, you pull that future closer, shaping your actions and decisions in the present.

Worldbuilding allows you to take charge of your own narrative, turning uncertainty into a landscape of possibility. By embracing your facets, setting clear boundaries, and navigating the chaos with intention, you crystallize your identity into something uniquely powerful and enduring.

Visioning Exercise 1: Dreaming Forward

Close your eyes and imagine yourself five years from now, having emerged from the IDENTITY GAP. Write a detailed vision of your future self, including:

- What does your life look like now that you've integrated all facets of your identity?

- How does your fully crystallized self navigate the world differently?

- What dreams have you brought into reality, and what steps did you take to get there?

Final Reflection

So, are you ready to explore the unknown and craft your future with intention? Your next chapter awaits, and the magic is already within you, waiting to be unleashed. Liminal thinking is your compass, and the diamond-like resilience within you will guide the way. Keep dreaming, keep crystallizing, and step boldly into your future.

Visioning Exercise 2: The Matrix of Identity

Imagine you're standing at a crossroads, like Neo in *The Matrix*. On one hand, you hold the blue pill—the comfort of the familiar, where you stay in the known reality of your old life. In the other, the red pill—the unknown, representing the leap into your new life with its new challenges, opportunities, and identity shifts. This is the ultimate liminal moment, where you decide whether to stay where you are or take the brave step into the unknown.

1. **The Red Pill vs. The Blue Pill:** Close your eyes and envision yourself holding the two pills.

   - **The Blue Pill**: If you were to stay in the familiar (whether physically or mentally), what would that look like? Imagine continuing your life as it is now. Consider the structure, routine, and identity of your old life. How does it feel? Safe? Predictable? Restrictive? What cognitive dissonance are you experiencing?

   - **The Red Pill**: Now, imagine taking the red pill. What does it look like on the other side of this transition into civilian life? Picture yourself navigating new landscapes—career, community, relationships. What challenges arise, but also, what opportunities are there for personal growth and freedom?

2. **Embrace the Liminal Space:** This transition is your liminal space—a period where old identities dissolve and new ones haven't fully formed. Reflect on how this in-between time might feel confusing, but it's also rich with potential.

Ask yourself:

- What can I bring from my old life into this new chapter?

- What part of my old identity no longer serves me, and how can I let it go?

- What is my old name, title, role?

- What new skills or mindsets do I need to thrive in civilian life?

3. **Write Your New Identity:** Take 10 minutes to journal:

   - What does my new identity look like on the other side of this transition?

   - What is my name, my title, my role?

   - What strengths do I carry with me?

   - What new opportunities excite me as I move forward?

After completing this exercise, you'll have clarity on what's holding you back, as well as a vision for who you want to become in your next life. You've embraced the discomfort of the liminal space and are now ready to crystallize a new identity that merges your experience with a future full of possibility. This process will help you step forward with courage and intention, leaving behind fear and uncertainty:

4. I, _____ (name), am 100% committed to a journey into the IDENTITY GAP to reinvent my new identity so I can live with alignment by _____ (date), so I can live the life of my dreams with integrity.

As Neo learned, the choice is always yours—take the red pill and let your new journey begin.

Visioning Exercise 3: Crossroads of the IDENTITY GAP

You are standing at the portal, a threshold between the past and the future. On the periphery of your vision, you see the outdated version of yourself—comfortable, familiar, and safe. You've lived in this space for so long, anchored in what is known. Glancing back, the pull to stay feels strong, urging you to decline the journey of transformation. Change *is uncertain*, and the path ahead is uncharted.

But before you lies the portal into *unfamiliar terrain*, shimmering with the potential for something greater. It's here, on the edges of the unknown, that your *magic* begins to awaken, where your true *essence* starts to *crystallize* into the person you are destined to become. The future beckons, calling you to step beyond the *periphery* of your old self and venture into a world of possibility, where your *dreams* take form, and your authentic self shines through.

You can stay rooted in the comfort of the past or take that first step into the unknown—where the new *you* begins to *manifest* with clarity and purpose. This is the space where transformation happens, not by playing it safe but by trusting in your inner *magician* and embracing the magic of the journey.

Will you remain in the periphery of who you were, or step boldly into who you're meant to become?

As we leave behind the concept of **Liminal Thinking**, where we explored the space between what was and what is becoming, we now step into the next chapter—**Brand Your New Identity**. Liminal spaces are often transitional, filled with uncertainty, but also with potential. It is in these moments that we have the greatest capacity for change, growth, and transformation.

Here, you aren't confined to the past, but you are empowered to create a future that aligns with your true self. The journey from uncertainty to clarity begins with acknowledging the void and using it as fertile ground to plant the seeds of who you want to become. Now, let's go with this momentum and focus on shaping, refining, and branding the identity that reflects your core values, desires, and purpose. This is where the creative process of identity-building begins in earnest. It's time to define and own your narrative.

CHAPTER 7
BRAND YOUR NEW IDENTITY

Crafting Your Brand: The Power of Personal and Professional Branding

In a world where identities are molded by constant change and growing competition, standing out isn't just an option; it's essential. But how do you rise above the noise? How do you make a lasting impact in a crowded field of voices and personalities? This is where personal and professional branding becomes crucial—a powerful process that allows you to craft your story and take charge of how others see and remember you.

What Is an Archetype?

An *archetype* is a universal symbol or pattern of behavior deeply ingrained in the human psyche. These archetypes, as defined by Carl Jung, represent common themes and characteristics found across cultures and time periods. They help us understand various aspects of ourselves and provide a framework for personal growth, storytelling, and identity formation. Archetypes such as the Hero, the Magician, and the Caregiver embody different facets of human experience and behavior, serving as powerful tools for shaping how we interact with the world and how we present ourselves.

In the context of branding, archetypes can help you align your personal and professional identity with a deeper narrative. Whether you resonate with the boldness of the Hero, the transformative power of the Magician, or the empathetic nature of the Caregiver, understanding your core archetype can guide how you communicate and connect with others.

Personal Branding: Uniquely You

Personal branding goes far beyond being a trendy buzzword; it's about telling the world exactly who you are, what you believe in, and why you matter. Think of it as the art of self-expression. Your personal brand is the emotional connection you create with others, whether through your actions, values, skills, or personality. It's the unique energy you bring into a room, the feelings you evoke, and the lasting impression you leave behind.

To build a personal brand that truly resonates, embrace self-discovery by asking, "What makes me unique? What do I offer that no one else can?" This authenticity is the cornerstone of a personal brand that not only inspires trust but also creates opportunities for growth, collaboration, and success. For instance, by embracing transformation and aligning with the Magician Archetype, you become the change you want to see in both you and the world around you.

But branding is not just about values—it's also about the physical representation of who you are. Appearance plays a key role in personal branding. Your wardrobe, grooming, body language, and color choices convey messages before you even say a word. Color psychology tells us that different shades evoke different emotions—wearing green can promote calmness, while yellow may convey optimism and energy. Choose clothing that aligns with the impression you want to make, and ensure your body language reflects confidence, openness, and professionalism. The way you carry yourself—whether standing tall or making eye contact—can say more about your personal brand than any resume.

Additionally, crafting a consistent online presence is essential. Your social media profiles, personal websites, and even your digital interactions should reflect the same message, tone, and values as your offline persona. Online, every post, picture, and comment becomes a reflection of your brand. Offline, the way you engage with others in conversations, meetings, and networking events solidifies that image. Consistency between your digital and physical worlds is key to building trust and authenticity.

Professional Branding: Your Identity in the Workplace

Your professional brand is how you position yourself in your career. It's about making a name for yourself, standing out as an expert in your field, and consistently highlighting the value you bring to your industry. This brand is built on not just what you do, but how you do it—how you approach challenges, collaborate with others, solve problems, and create innovative solutions.

Verbal and nonverbal communication are key aspects of professional branding. How you speak, the tone of your voice, and the words you choose all send signals about your professionalism and credibility. But nonverbal communication, such as gestures, facial expressions, and posture, is just as crucial. You can be saying all the right things, but if your body language doesn't match, it can send mixed messages.

Furthermore, your resume and cover letter act as the first introduction to your professional brand. The language and tone you use should not only be professional but should also reflect your personality and the values you stand for. These documents are your opportunity to showcase your strengths and communicate what sets you apart from other candidates. Your speech patterns, whether formal or conversational, and your ability to articulate ideas clearly, further solidify the image of a competent and confident professional.

The way you communicate in person or online plays a significant role in building credibility. When people interact with you, every conversation becomes part of your brand narrative. Whether you're speaking with a colleague, manager, or potential client, you're continuously shaping their perception of who you are and what you stand for.

Your offline presence in the workplace also contributes significantly to your brand. The way you interact with others in meetings, the way you carry yourself during presentations, and even your punctuality all help to establish a reputation. It's important to be intentional in these moments to ensure your professional brand reflects the values and qualities you want others to associate with you.

The Intersection of Personal and Professional Branding

While personal and professional branding may seem like two distinct areas, they are deeply intertwined. Your personal values, beliefs, and passions often shape how you behave professionally. For instance, if your personal brand aligns with the Lover Archetype, where connection, empathy, and building relationships are core values, it will naturally influence how you collaborate with colleagues and clients. You may be more collaborative, compassionate, and focused on creating harmonious work environments.

It's essential that both your personal and professional brands are in harmony. Consistency across all platforms—from how you dress to how you speak, whether online or offline—builds credibility and trust. If your personal and professional personas are at odds, it creates confusion for others, and people may question the authenticity of your brand.

The key to mastering this balance lies in ensuring your personal brand aligns with your professional aspirations. For example, if you want to position yourself as a leader in your industry, your personal brand should reflect traits like confidence, decisiveness, and integrity.

Strategies to Build Your 55% -Professional Identity

1. **Define Your Mission and Vision:** Your mission statement should reflect your deepest values and function as a compass that guides all your decisions and actions. Who are you becoming? What do you stand for?

2. **Leverage Your Strengths:** Use tools like Clifton Strengths, MBTI, or the Enneagram to identify your core talents. These insights can help you focus on areas where you naturally excel, positioning you as an expert in your niche.

3. **Build a Consistent Visual and Verbal Identity:** From your wardrobe choices to your email signature, every detail should reflect the values and image you want to project. Make sure your online and offline presence are aligned.

4. **Network with Intent:** Build meaningful connections with those who align with your mission. Engage in communities that challenge and inspire you to grow. Relationships are the backbone of professional success.

5. **Showcase Thought Leadership:** Share your insights through blog posts, articles, public speaking, and engaging in relevant discussions. Being seen as a thought leader increases your visibility and influence within your field.

Visibility: How to Make Your Brand Shine

Visibility is key to establishing a brand, but it's not about being everywhere at once. Instead, focus on being in the right places where your voice will resonate the most. Carefully curate your social media content to reflect your personal and professional values. Share stories, accomplishments, and lessons learned that align with your brand.

Equally important is your offline presence. How you present yourself in face-to-face interactions, at networking events, and even in having casual conversations with colleagues can make a significant difference in how your brand is perceived. When you're visible in the right ways and places, opportunities begin to open.

Your Brand, Your Power

Crafting a personal and professional brand is about more than just standing out—it's about defining how the world experiences you. It's the power to shape your identity, attract the right opportunities, and build a network of meaningful connections. This journey is ongoing, and your brand will evolve with you. By aligning both your personal and professional brands, you take control of your narrative and ensure your presence is felt in ways that are both authentic and impactful.

As you conclude the process of branding your new identity, it's essential to remember that identity is not a static construct. Just like diamonds are formed under immense pressure, the value and strength of your identity are often forged in moments of chaos and uncertainty. This transition leads us to the next chapter — *Power in Chaos*—where we'll explore how, like a diamond shaped by Earth's forces, our truest selves emerge from the turbulence and challenges life throws at us.

While branding provides structure and clarity, chaos is the unpredictable forge where your identity is tested and refined. It reminds us that, at our core, we are earthlings—adaptable, resilient, and ever-evolving. In the coming chapter, we will delve into how embracing the unpredictable, like a diamond embracing pressure, can reveal the brilliance of who you are becoming.

As we journey further, consider this: your value isn't just in the identity you shape deliberately, but in how you navigate the unknown.

FROM CHAOS TO VICTORY: A JOURNEY OF GROWTH

In the heart of chaos, where shadows dance,
We find the seeds of change, a sacred chance.
Facets of our being, rough and unrefined,
Cut by life's sharp edge, where we are blind.

Diamonds form in darkness, deep within the stone,
Each flaw a map to paths we've never known.
Pressure builds and breaks what once we knew,
But in those shattered pieces, something new.

The storm that shakes the ground beneath our feet,
Transforms the solid earth, where we meet.
Old selves fall away, like autumn leaves,
Making room for growth, as nature weaves.

Victory is born not from the gentle sway,
But from the tempest, night turned into day.
We rise from ashes, forged by fire's light,
Wings of strength unfurl, taking flight.

Change is not a burden, but a gift in disguise,
In chaos, we find the spark that never dies.
Each moment of growth, a diamond bright,
Polished by our journey, shining in the night.

So embrace the struggle, the fractures of your soul,
For they are the patterns that make you whole.
From chaos to victory, the path we trace,
Leads us to the brilliance of our own grace.

CHAPTER 8
POWER IN CHAOS

In times of chaos, optimism can be your greatest power. The famous parable, "There must be a pony somewhere," embodies this mindset. The story goes that two children are given piles of manure to sort through. While one despairs, the other digs with enthusiasm, believing that with so much manure, there must be a pony somewhere. This tale illustrates the power of perspective—where one sees only problems, the other sees opportunity. In the face of adversity, adopting this optimistic outlook allows us to find hidden possibilities and maintain hope. As Viktor Frankl suggested in *Man's Search for Meaning*, finding purpose even in suffering can transform our experience and give us the strength to persevere. Let optimism be your guiding light, turning chaos into a pathway for growth.

The Journey into Chaos

Chaos, derived from the Greek word 'khaos,' signifies a 'gap' or 'nothingness.' Within this gap lies the power of creation. To navigate through this void, envision yourself as an astronaut embarking on a deep space mission of exploration. Embrace an attitude of openness and curiosity, much like a rocket preparing for liftoff. To achieve this lift-off, it's essential to release the chaos and burdens that hold you back. Just as a rocket breaks free from Earth's atmosphere, you, too, can clear the way and shatter the barriers that obstruct your dreams. By creating the necessary space, you open yourself up to exploring your inner frontiers and crafting the life you've always envisioned.

Imagine looking into a mirror and seeing fragments of who you used to be. Trauma can feel like a shattered reflection, distorting your sense of self and leaving you in a liminal, surreal, dreamlike state. Chaos often appears as an unwelcome guest in our lives, arriving unexpectedly, disrupting the familiar, and challenging our sense of self. Whether it's a trauma that shatters our world, a moral injury that makes us question our values, or the insidious erosion of self from narcissistic abuse, chaos is the fertile ground from which we can rediscover who we truly are. Burnout, too, creeps in quietly, one stage at a time, until we find ourselves standing at the edge, staring into the void. Yet, within this turmoil lies a hidden power—an opportunity to reclaim ourselves, to rediscover our essence, and to emerge more aligned with our deepest values.

Identity Loss from Trauma

Trauma can strip away our sense of identity like a tidal wave, leaving us feeling raw, exposed, and uncertain. This loss is more than a psychological wound; it is a fragmentation of the self, where pieces of who we thought we were scattered into the chaos of survival. Whether we face sudden loss, abuse, betrayal, or a violent event, trauma often brings with it a sense of disorientation and numbness.

The Magician's archetype understands that chaos is not the end but a critical initiation. By confronting the shadows of our past and the depths of our pain, we have the chance to alchemize suffering into wisdom, to transmute darkness into light. This journey is not linear but cyclical, requiring the courage to face our inner demons and the fortitude to reconstruct ourselves piece by piece.

Moral Injury: A Rift in the Soul

Moral injury occurs when our actions—or inactions—violate our deeply held beliefs and ethical codes. It is the guilt of the soldier who pulled the trigger, the nurse who couldn't save everyone, or the whistleblower whose truth-telling brought down colleagues. It is an invisible wound that cuts to the core of our moral identity, leaving us questioning our worth and purpose.

The Magician's path teaches us that moral injury is a crucible for transformation. In this alchemical process, we burn away the guilt and shame, distilling from our pain the essence of our true values and purpose. The journey toward healing involve integrating these painful experiences into a new narrative of who we are, one that honors both the shadow and the light within us.

Career Trauma: Losing Your 55%

Career trauma can manifest in many forms—being underemployed, unemployed, trapped in a toxic work environment, or feeling unsupported by your community in your business and employment endeavors. It might be the result of losing a significant portion of your professional identity—like losing 55% of what once defined you. This loss can leave you feeling adrift, undervalued, and uncertain about the future.

But what if that 55% was not lost forever but simply waiting to be rediscovered, refined, and realigned? At this pivotal moment, you can fill in those gaps, reclaim your professional worth, and find a new alignment that resonates with your true self. The key is to approach this process with the understanding that this 55% is not just a number but a part of your identity that deserves to be valued and protected like a rare diamond.

To achieve this, consider resources that can guide you in reinventing yourself after career trauma. Professional development courses, networking events, career coaching, and mentorship programs can help you regain confidence and clarity. Utilize online platforms to expand your skills, connect with industry leaders, and explore new opportunities. Seeking therapy or support groups can also help process the emotional impact of career setbacks, while financial planning services can offer practical steps for managing the economic toll of unemployment or underemployment.

Don't get stuck in a job that feels like a dead end. Instead, embrace this time to pivot towards something more fulfilling. Your 55% is your core—the part of you that knows your value, your passion, and your purpose. Protect it fiercely and use it as a foundation to rebuild, refocus, and realign. Remember, like a diamond, your career identity is multifaceted and resilient, capable of withstanding pressure and emerging stronger and more brilliant than before.

Narcissistic Abuse: The Erosion of Self

Narcissistic abuse is like a slow-acting poison, a rabbit hole of no return silently eroding one's sense of self over time. It is the constant gaslighting, manipulation, and emotional exploitation that undermines our confidence and warps our reality. In these relationships, the narcissist becomes the sun, and we revolve around them, losing our own center. The cycle of idealization, devaluation, and discard leaves us feeling unworthy, invisible, and deeply lost.

NARCISSUS: DESTROYER OF DREAMS

In the garden's mirrored pool so still,
A youth beheld his form, a beauty's thrill.
Narcissus, fair, with eyes like stars aglow,
Gazed deep, entranced by what he didn't know.

A face reflected in the waters' grace,
A dream, a vision, in that crystal space.
He reached, he yearned, but could not touch the gleam,
For love itself had turned into a dream.

The pool, a canvas of illusions cast,
Held him captive, bound to shadows vast.
In endless trance, he watched his own demise,
A heart of stone beneath those wistful eyes.

No mortal heart could hold such sweet delight,
For beauty's prison chains the soul in plight.
What dreams he had, now faded in despair,
As endless love turned into empty air.

Oh, Narcissus, in your endless, vain retreat,
You've shattered dreams, made love's sweet song replete.
In your reflection, lies a silent scream,
The beauty lost, the destroyer of dreams.

The Magician within us knows that power lies in reclaiming our narrative, breaking free from the illusion of the narcissist's control, and rediscovering our intrinsic worth. This process often involves setting firm boundaries, engaging in deep self-reflection, and reconnecting with our core values and passions. It is about remembering that we are the creators of our reality, not mere spectators in someone else's drama.

Burnout: The Slow Descent into Oblivion

Burnout is often misunderstood as mere exhaustion, but it is much more insidious. It is the slow, creeping descent into apathy, cynicism, and detachment from the very things that once gave our lives meaning. Christina Maslach and her colleagues identified twelve stages of burnout, starting from the compulsion to prove oneself, through neglect of personal needs, withdrawal, and depersonalization, ending in total mental and physical collapse.

To navigate burnout, we must engage in the Magician's work of self-restoration and renewal. It begins with recognizing where we are in the burnout process, understanding how we got there, and daring to ask, "What is this burnout revealing about my deepest values, my neglected passions, my unlived dreams?" The journey back involves setting new boundaries, reimagining our priorities, and cultivating practices that nurture our soul.

Stoic Wisdom for Navigating Career Chaos and Trauma

Stoic wisdom offers valuable insights for those experiencing chaos and trauma in their careers. Stoicism, a philosophy founded in ancient Greece, teaches that while we cannot control external events, we can control our responses. This approach is particularly powerful in times of professional turmoil when chaos and uncertainty may seem overwhelming.

One of the key Stoic principles is the distinction between what is within our control and what is not. Marcus Aurelius, a Roman emperor, and Stoic philosopher, wrote, "You have power over your mind—not outside events. Realize this, and you will find strength." By focusing on our internal state—our thoughts, attitudes, and actions—we can maintain clarity amid career turbulence. This perspective helps us navigate workplace trauma, such as layoffs, conflicts, or unexpected changes, by emphasizing resilience and personal growth over circumstances we cannot change.

Stoicism also encourages us to view challenges as opportunities for growth, much like how a diamond forms under pressure. Each challenge can be a facet of our personal development, polishing our character and revealing our inner strength. The Stoic practice of "amor fati" or "love of fate" suggests embracing all events, including difficulties, as part of our journey. This acceptance transforms obstacles into stepping stones toward a more resilient and adaptable self.

Additionally, Stoicism aligns with the heroic journey, where every hero or heroine faces trials and adversity to achieve victory. By embodying the virtues of courage, wisdom, and self-discipline, we become the hero of our own career story, moving from a place of chaos to one of clarity and purpose.

In times of career uncertainty or trauma, Stoic wisdom offers a path to victory through inner strength and balanced perspective, helping us navigate life's inevitable upheavals with grace and resolve.

Unshackling Shame

"Unshackling Shame" is a powerful call to action for both women and men to break free from the chains of societal conditioning that have long perpetuated feelings of inadequacy and guilt. For too long, women have been burdened by shame— whether it stems from unrealistic expectations, historical injustices, or the age-old fear of being cast out. This shame not only stifles women's potential but also restricts men, who are often trapped in traditional roles that dictate how they should express vulnerability and support.

Liberation begins with recognizing that letting go of shame creates a space for healing and transformation. In a crystallized union of understanding, we can dismantle the oppressive narratives of the past, from the witch hunts to the systemic exclusion that has persisted through generations. This act of unshackling isn't about reclaiming power for only women; it's a collective journey that invites men to participate in redefining strength and support.

In this journey from victimhood to victory, both the hero and the heroine find their voices, empowering each other to rise above chaos. The power within chaos is not merely destruction but the potential for rebirth and renewal. By embracing this transformative process, we foster a culture that celebrates authenticity and compassion, enabling everyone to thrive. It is time to unshackle shame, for in that liberation lies the strength to build a brighter, more equitable future for all.

Recovering Your Self: The Magician's Alchemy

The process of recovery begins with a courageous act of self-examination. The Magician archetype teaches us that even in our darkest moments, we hold the key to our liberation. The power is not outside us, but within. Make trauma your superpower.

1. **Awareness and Acceptance:** Recognize and accept the reality of your situation. Understand that chaos is not a flaw, but an integral part of growth. Embrace your current state without judgment, knowing that every broken piece of your identity can be a source of transformation.

2. **Radical Self-Compassion:** Extend compassion to yourself as you would to a dear friend. Understand that your pain, confusion, and suffering are part of the human experience. Practice self-kindness in your thoughts, words, and actions. Reaffirm your worthiness regardless of external circumstances.

3. **Reclaim Your Narrative:** Reframe your story from victim to survivor, from passive participant to active creator. Identify the moments in your journey that have shaped you, and re-author them with the lens of resilience, strength, and wisdom gained.

4. **Find Meaning in Chaos:** As Viktor Frankl reminds us in Man's Search for Meaning, even in the most harrowing sit-

uations, we have the power to choose our response. Seek meaning in your suffering. Ask yourself, "What can I learn from this? How can I grow? What purpose can emerge from this pain?"

5. **Reconnect with Your Core Values:** Identify and affirm your core values. Use them as your North Star to navigate through the uncertainty. Align your decisions, actions, and boundaries with these values to rebuild a more authentic and empowered self.

6. **Create Rituals for Renewal:** Establish rituals that nourish your spirit, mind, and body. Meditation, journaling, creative expression, and time in nature can help ground you and re-connect you with your inner Magician, the source of your personal power.

Finding Meaning and Support: Embracing the Journey

The journey through chaos is not one to be walked alone. Lean into your support systems—friends, family, therapists, and support groups. Consider spiritual or philosophical teachings that resonate with you. Embrace the tools and practices that help you reconnect with your inner wisdom, like mindfulness, cognitive behavioral therapy, or somatic practices.

Remember, as Viktor Frankl taught, even in the most desperate of circumstances, we retain the freedom to choose our attitude. By reclaiming this choice, we reclaim our power.

Rebirth from the Ashes

Just as the phoenix rises from its ashes, we, too, can emerge from the chaos of trauma, moral injury, narcissistic abuse, and burnout stronger, wiser, and more aligned with our true selves. The journey into chaos is a rite of passage, an initiation into a deeper understanding of who we are. The power is within us to transform pain into purpose, suffering into strength, and chaos into clarity.

Discover a wide range of archetypes to explore for depth and narrative coaching insights by visiting **www.elysiandream.net.**

As we have explored the transformative potential of chaos, it becomes clear that the turbulent forces of our lives can forge new paths and reveal hidden strengths. Yet, the journey does not end with surviving the storms. It leads us to a deeper, more profound challenge—one that calls us to confront our inner landscape and bridge *The Heroic IDENTITY GAP*. This gap is where we close the distance between who is a hero. Chaos may shape us, but *The Heroic IDENTITY GAP* is where we dive deeper into the exploration of self and choose to find hidden strengths and transform not just our circumstances but ourselves. Now, we step into the heart of the journey—the pursuit of becoming the hero of your own life.

HEROINE

In the depths of shadow, a quiet spark,
A whispering dream that dances in the dark.
A heartbeats' rhythm, a steady drum,
The hero waits, for the time to come.

Shattered glass reflects the sky,
Fragments glint like stars on high,
Each piece a facet, each cut a scar,
A diamond forming where we are.

Invisible threads weave the days,
The roles we play, the debts we pay.
Yet within, a voice calls strong and clear,
To break the mold and cast off fear.

Through the glass, with fists of light,
Breaking through to claim our right.
A victor rising, bold and true,
Emerges bright from shadowed view.

From unseen depths, to rise and climb,
To shape our fate and own our time.
A diamond forged, with facets bright,
From invisible shadow, into the light.

A hero's journey, a path unknown,
From glass and darkness, we carve our throne.
Facets glisten, as dreams take flight,
From hidden corners, into the light.

The gap is crossed, the mask is shed,
We speak the words once left unsaid.
Heroic identity, a victor here,
No longer hidden, but shining clear.

CHAPTER 9
THE HEROIC IDENTITY GAP

Emerging from the Shadows: Embracing the Antihero Syndrome and Shifting the Narrative

Imagine a world where heroism is not confined to the pages of mythological epics or the screens of blockbuster movies. Picture a new paradigm where the true essence of heroism is illuminated not by grandiose gestures, but by the quiet, powerful acts of everyday women. This shift from the traditional heroic narrative to a more inclusive and nuanced understanding is crucial in addressing what we call "Antihero Syndrome."

Understanding Antihero Syndrome: Women in the Shadow of Traditional Heroism

Antihero Syndrome describes the struggle women face when their contributions and qualities are overshadowed by the traditional, often male-centric, archetype of heroism. This archetype celebrates traits such as physical strength, boldness, and solitary triumphs—qualities that, while significant, do not encompass the full spectrum of heroism. Women who excel in empathy, collaboration, and inner strength may feel diminished or invisible when their achievements do not align with these conventional ideals.

The societal pressure to fit into this heroic mold can lead to a sense of inadequacy, as women often feel they need to conform to a standard that does not reflect their true strengths. Yet, it is essential to recognize that heroism can manifest in diverse ways—ways that may not always align with traditional narratives but are nonetheless powerful and significant.

Shattering Stereotypes: Celebrating the Unseen Heroes

Let's challenge the conventional notion of heroism by highlighting those whose bravery and impact are often overlooked. Women like Malala Yousafzai, who championed education despite extreme adversity, and countless others who juggle multiple roles with grace, redefine what it means to be a hero. Their stories demonstrate that heroism is not confined to dramatic rescues or epic battles; it is present in the everyday acts of courage and resilience that shape our world in profound ways.

Broadening Our Definition of Heroism

Traditional heroism often emphasizes dramatic feats and public accolades, missing the quieter forms of courage demonstrated daily by women. For example, Malala Yousafzai's advocacy for education in the face of life-threatening opposition showcases that true heroism involves standing up against injustice and fighting for fundamental rights (Yousafzai & Lamb, 2013). Similarly, women managing the complex demands of family, career, and personal growth exhibit heroism through their perseverance and dedication (Hochschild & Machung, 2012).

By expanding our definition of heroism to include these everyday acts of bravery, we foster a more inclusive understanding of strength and resilience. Recognizing and celebrating the diverse ways women contribute to society challenges outdated stereotypes and inspires future generations to value different forms of courage.

Stoic Wisdom for Equality

Stoic wisdom emphasizes the inherent equality of all human beings, grounded in the belief that virtue, reason, and moral character are what define a person—not their gender or social status. Stoic philosophers like Musonius Rufus, one of the few ancient Stoics who explicitly discussed women's education, argued that women are equally capable of pursuing virtue and wisdom as men. He advocated for women's education and the cultivation of their intellect, noting that since both men and women possess the same rational soul, they should be given the same opportunities to develop their virtues.

For Stoics, justice and equality are rooted in the idea that every individual has the potential for moral excellence. Epictetus and Marcus Aurelius remind us that what truly matters is how we live according to virtue and wisdom, not superficial distinctions. This perspective supports equality and dismisses societal roles or limitations placed on women.

Navigating the Heroic IDENTITY GAP

Many women experience a "Heroic IDENTITY GAP," an internal conflict between their self-perception and societal expectations of heroism. This gap often leads to role confusion, doing it all, imposter syndrome, and moral dilemmas. Women may feel torn between traditional expectations and their personal aspirations, struggling to reconcile their desires with the roles society imposes upon them.

To bridge this gap, women must redefine heroism on their own terms. Heroism is not just about grand achievements or the absence of fear; it is about facing challenges with authenticity and resilience. Embracing these qualities aligns with the Magician archetype, which seeks to transform and inspire (Gilligan, 1982).

Empowering Women: Breaking Through Invisibility

While many women feel invisible, women veterans often face a profound sense of invisibility as they transition from military to civilian life. Despite their valuable skills and experiences, they frequently encounter stereotypes and biases that undermine their contributions. Addressing this invisibility requires a concerted effort to support their transition, employment, or business and recognize and value their achievements.

The Silent Struggle: Understanding Antihero Syndrome

In the grand narrative of heroism, the spotlight often shines on the traditional, male-dominated archetype—think of the solitary warrior or the bold adventurer. This archetype glorifies traits like physical strength and daring feats, leaving little room for the nuanced, collaborative heroism that women frequently embody. Antihero Syndrome occurs when women feel the pressure to conform to these masculine ideals, only to find that their own heroic qualities, such as empathy, collaboration, and inner resilience, are undervalued or overlooked.

This syndrome can manifest in several ways:

1. **Invisibility**: Women often experience a profound sense of being overlooked, especially in professional or social contexts where their contributions are not fully recognized. For women veterans, this can mean their military service and skills are undervalued in civilian life. (National Center for Women & Veterans' Health, 2021).

2. **Role Confusion**: When societal expectations conflict with personal aspirations, women may struggle to define their roles. They may feel torn between traditional expectations of nurturing and support and their own desires to lead and take risks.

3. **Imposter Syndrome**: This feeling of inadequacy, despite evident achievements, is especially prevalent among women. They may doubt their worthiness of the "hero" label and feel like frauds, particularly in environments where female representation is sparse. (Gilligan, 1982).

Embracing Heroism Beyond the Conventional

Heroism can be redefined to include the everyday acts of bravery demonstrated by women. This means recognizing and valuing:

- **Courage in Advocacy**: Malala Yousafzai's fight for girls' education shows that heroism involves standing up against injustice and challenging oppressive norms.

- **Strength in Daily Life**: Women who manage households, careers, and personal growth reflect a form of heroism rooted in resilience and dedication, despite not receiving public accolades.

Shining Beyond the Shadow: Embracing the Heroic Potential in Every Woman

Imagine a world where true heroism is not confined to mythical quests or grand public gestures but is instead found in the everyday courage of women who navigate their lives with quiet strength and resilience. Unfortunately, many women find themselves grappling with what I call "Antihero Syndrome," a challenge where traditional heroic ideals overshadow their unique strengths and achievements. This phenomenon can be particularly pronounced in women veterans, whose contributions are often undervalued or unseen. Let's explore how women can transcend these limitations, redefine heroism, and embrace their true potential.

Reclaiming Your Heroic Identity

To overcome Antihero Syndrome and reclaim your heroic identity, consider the following strategies:

1. **Redefine Heroism**: Expand your definition of heroism to include the quiet, everyday acts of courage and strength that you and other women exhibit. Recognize that true bravery is often found in resilience, perseverance, and the ability to inspire and support others.

2. **Address Role Confusion**: Reflect on your personal values and aspirations. Embrace roles that align with your vision of heroism, even if they diverge from traditional expectations.

3. **Combat Imposter Syndrome**: Challenge your inner critic by acknowledging your achievements and strengths. Surround yourself with supportive mentors and peers who can validate your contributions and build your confidence.

4. **Increase Visibility for Women Veterans**: Advocate for greater recognition of women veterans' contributions. Support initiatives that promote their achievements and create inclusive environments where their skills are valued. (Women Veterans Alliance, 2023).

5. **Build Inclusive Support Systems**: Engage with organizations and communities that provide tailored support for women veterans, addressing their unique needs and helping them transition successfully into civilian roles (VA, 2022).

Heroism extends far beyond traditional narratives of grandeur and is not a one-size-fits-all concept. By broadening our understanding to include the diverse ways in which women demonstrate bravery and resilience, we can create a more inclusive and equitable view of heroism. Recognizing and celebrating the everyday heroism of women—whether they are on the battlefield or managing the complexities of daily life—ensures that all forms of strength and courage are valued. Let's honor all forms of strength and ensure that every contribution, whether visible or not, is celebrated and valued.

In the next chapter, ***Heroic Wisdom***, we'll dive into the ancient teachings and philosophies that have guided countless heroes throughout history. By understanding the Hero Archetype, as depicted in myths and legends from various cultures, we'll uncover how ancient wisdom offers timeless strategies for overcoming challenges and embodying resilience. These traditions emphasize the balance between strength and humility, courage, and compassion, shaping a hero's journey that transcends time. Here, we'll explore how these insights can apply to your own life, helping you navigate your path with clarity and purpose.

CHAPTER 10
HEROIC WISDOM

Unleashing Your Inner Hero: Empowering Women to Reclaim Their Heroic Potential

Ever felt like the world's hero narrative just does not fit you? Have you felt overshadowed, struggled with self-doubt, or faced roles that diluted your true potential? It is time to rewrite the script. As a life coach, my mission is to guide you through this transformative journey, helping you redefine and embrace your unique heroic identity.

Redefine Heroism: Embrace the Everyday Bravery

Heroism is not just about epic battles or dramatic rescues. It is about the courage you show in everyday challenges. Start by challenging the traditional notions of heroism. Recognize that true bravery can be found in small, consistent acts of courage— whether it is standing up for yourself, navigating life's difficulties, or making tough decisions. By expanding your view of heroism, you will start to see your own heroic qualities more clearly.

Seek Out Role Models: Find Inspiration and Create Your Own

Look for or create role models who reflect the diverse forms of heroism you aspire to. This could mean exploring the lives of mythological heroines, modern-day trailblazers, or historical figures who broke the mold. Let their stories inspire you and show you what is possible. And do not be afraid to become a role model yourself, demonstrating what it means to be heroic in your own way.

Embrace Vulnerability: The Power of Authenticity

Heroism involves more than just strength—it includes vulnerability and authenticity. Embrace your struggles and imperfections as integral parts of your journey. Understanding that vulnerability can be a source of strength allows you to connect more deeply with others and empowers you to face challenges with greater courage.

Integrate Stoic Wisdom: Harness Ancient Principles for Modern Challenges

Stoicism, the ancient philosophy of inner strength and resilience, offers powerful tools for navigating life's transitions. By integrating Stoic principles into your life, you can build a heroic identity grounded in virtue and clarity. Here is how:

1. **Cultivate Resilience: Focus on What You Can Control** Stoicism teaches us to accept what we cannot change and to concentrate on what we can control. Develop resilience by embracing life's challenges and learning from them. When faced with obstacles, ask yourself: "What can I control in this situation? How can I use this experience to grow?"

2. **Practice Mindfulness: Stay Present and Engaged** Stoics emphasize living in the present moment. Keep your focus on the here and now rather than dwelling on past regrets or future anxieties. Practicing mindfulness helps you

stay grounded and makes you more effective in managing life's demands.

3. **Exercise Reason and Wisdom: Make Thoughtful Decisions** Stoicism encourages rational thinking and self-reflection. When confronted with decisions, use reason to guide your actions. Strive for clarity and objectivity, and consider how your choices align with your core values.

4. **Manage Emotions: Respond Thoughtfully** While emotions are natural, Stoics advocate for maintaining emotional balance. Rather than letting emotions drive your actions, respond thoughtfully. This approach helps you stay calm and focused, even in stressful situations.

5. **Focus on Virtue: Live by Core Principles** Embrace Stoic virtues such as courage, wisdom, justice, and temperance. Let these virtues guide your actions and interactions, providing a solid foundation for your heroic journey.

6. **Embrace Adversity: View Challenges as Opportunities** Stoicism teaches that obstacles can lead to growth. When facing adversity, view it as an opportunity to gain experience and improve. This mindset transforms challenges into stepping stones toward greater personal development.

7. **Practice Gratitude: Appreciate What You Have** Gratitude is a key aspect of Stoicism. Reflect on the positives in your life and express thanks. This practice helps you stay humble and centered, enhancing your overall sense of well-being.

Engage in Self-Reflection: Align Actions with Values

Regularly reflect on your actions and decisions. Consider how they align with your values and goals. This self-awareness ensures that you remain true to your authentic self, even as you navigate change.

Live with Purpose: Align Goals with Meaning

Identify your purpose and align your actions with it. A clear sense of purpose provides direction and motivation, helping you stay focused on your heroic journey.

Prepare for Change: Embrace Life's Flux

Expect and accept change as a natural part of life. Embracing change with flexibility allows you to adapt and thrive in the face of uncertainty.

Harness the Hero Archetype: Voice, Colors, and Imagery

To fully embody your heroic potential, align with the Hero archetype's characteristics. This includes embracing your unique voice, colors, and imagery that reflect your heroic identity.

- **Heroic Voice:** Develop a voice that resonates with your values and mission. This could be assertive, compassionate, or visionary—whatever aligns with your true self.

- **Heroic Colors and Imagery:** Use colors and imagery that evoke strength and courage. For example, deep blues and bold reds can represent bravery, while empowering symbols and images can reinforce your identity as a hero.

- **Creative Visualization:** Design a personal emblem or symbol that represents your heroic journey. Incorporate colors and imagery that inspire you and reflect your core values.

Heroic Visualization: Embracing Your Inner Hero

Go to **elysiandream.net** to listen to this meditation.

Find a quiet space where you can relax without distractions. Sit comfortably or lie down, and take a few deep breaths, inhaling slowly through your nose and exhaling through your mouth. Let the tension in your body melt away with each breath. Close your eyes and allow yourself to drift into a state of calm and focus.

Imagine yourself standing at the edge of a vast, ancient forest. The trees tower above you, their leaves glowing with a golden light as they sway gently in the breeze. The scent of pine, earth, and distant rain fills the air, grounding you to the moment. You feel a cool, invigorating breeze on your skin, carrying with it a sense of anticipation. This forest is both mysterious and welcoming— representing the uncharted path of your heroic journey.

As you step forward into the forest, you feel a transformation. A hero's cloak, woven with deep colors and adorned with symbols of courage, integrity, and resilience, drapes over your shoulders. The weight of this cloak is reassuring, a reminder of the strength you carry within. A soft hum of energy pulses through the fabric, connecting you to your deepest self, grounding you in your purpose. With each step, your posture becomes more confident, your gaze steadier, and your movements deliberate. You embody the presence of a hero— strong, determined, and filled with quiet confidence.

The path before you is winding, but bathed in a soft, glowing light that symbolizes your inner wisdom and intuition. As you walk, you can hear the gentle rustle of leaves underfoot, the distant call of birds overhead, and the rhythmic beating of your heart—steady and sure, a reminder of your resilience.

Soon, you come to a clearing where symbols of strength and leadership appear before you—a sword for courage, a shield for protection, a crown for wisdom, and a torch for guiding others. You pick up each item, feeling their weight in your hands, knowing they represent the qualities you possess: the courage to face challenges, the integrity to act with honor, and the resilience to rise even after hardship.

Along your path, you encounter figures that embody the traits of your inner hero. A wise mentor, their gaze steady and compassionate, offers you wisdom—reminding you that leadership is not about control, but about self-sacrifice and acting with purpose. A courageous ally steps forward, showing you that facing challenges head-on with determination and compassion for others is the way forward. And finally, a phoenix rises from the ashes, symbolizing your own ability to transform, to heal, and to rise above betrayal, guilt, and shame.

As you continue walking, you encounter obstacles—large boulders, thick vines, and dark shadows. These represent the challenges you have faced, the fear of failure, the wounds of loss and betrayal. But with each step, you feel the cloak of your hero's identity wrapping you in strength. You navigate each obstacle with calm determination, your sword cutting through the vines, your shield protecting you from fear, your crown guiding your decisions with wisdom, and your torch lighting the way forward. You move with purpose, overcoming each trial as you lean into your leadership, resilience, and courage.

In the distance, you hear the soft trickle of water, a stream flowing peacefully, representing the balance and peace you seek. The scent of the water mixes with the earthy tones of the forest, reminding you that amidst the chaos, there is always a place of calm within. As you approach the stream, you pause to reflect. You think of the people you seek to protect, the goals you aim to achieve, and the desires you long to fulfill—understanding, healing, connection, and restoration. These are the driving forces behind your journey.

Finally, you reach a brilliant clearing bathed in warm, golden light. The air is still, calm, and filled with a sense of accomplishment. This is your sanctuary, the space of ultimate achievement. As you stand here, you take a deep breath and feel the fullness of your journey— the trials, the growth, and the transformation. You have overcome, you have led, and you have become more than you imagined.

As you prepare to leave this sacred space and return to your daily life, you feel the weight of your heroic cloak resting on your shoulders once more. It is lighter now, but its power remains. You carry the strength of the sword, the protection of the shield, the wisdom of the crown, the guidance of the torch, and the transformation of the phoenix. These are not just symbols—they are a part of you, ready to guide you in every moment.

Take a few deep breaths, bringing your awareness back to the present. Wiggle your fingers and toes, and gently open your eyes. The sounds of the forest slowly fade, replaced by the steady rhythm of your breath and the sense of calm that now envelops you.

Carry the strength, clarity, and courage of your heroic self with you, knowing that whatever challenges lie ahead, you have the power within to face them. Embrace your journey, and let your inner hero lead you toward your greatest aspirations.

Your Heroic Journey Awaits

Reclaiming your heroic identity is a transformative process that involves redefining heroism, seeking inspiration, embracing vulnerability, and integrating Stoic wisdom. By harnessing the Hero archetype and using its principles to guide your journey, you can navigate life's transitions with confidence and purpose. Remember, true heroism is found in both grand and everyday acts of courage.

Embrace your unique path and step boldly into the life you are meant to lead. The path to reclaiming your heroic identity is a deeply personal journey that involves redefining heroism, finding inspiring role models, embracing vulnerability, and integrating Stoic wisdom into your life. By adopting these strategies, you can navigate life's transitions with confidence, purpose, and resilience. Remember, true heroism lies not just in grand deeds but in the everyday courage and strength you embody. Embrace your unique heroism and step boldly into the life you are meant to lead.

Now that you have a foundation in Heroic Wisdom and can channel your inner hero, it's time to deepen this journey. In the next chapter, *Hero Unchained*, we'll explore the integration of masculine and feminine energies—the powerful union that expands your heroic potential. Through this lens, we'll examine how balancing these forces brings a richer, more harmonious approach to overcoming life's challenges and crafting your unique path forward. Prepare to uncover new dimensions within, where both strength and compassion, assertiveness and intuition come together to create an unbreakable foundation for growth and transformation.

HERO UNCHAINED

Unchained from the roles that once confined,
A hero's spirit is now refined.
No longer bound by shadowed chains,
In newfound freedom, a light remains.

Divine energies, harmoniously blend,
A cosmic dance where opposites mend.
Strength and grace in perfect accord,
Peace and power, a unified chord.

In the balance of day and night,
The hero's heart finds its light.
A symphony of discord resolved,
In union's embrace, all problems dissolved.

The struggles of old now softly fade,
In the calm of balance, serenely laid.
Harmony flows through every vein,
A tranquil soul, unburdened by pain.

No longer fragmented, no longer torn,
A hero reborn in peace, adorned.
In divine balance, the soul does find,
A timeless harmony, perfectly aligned.

So let the hero's journey be one of grace,
A dance of energies in sacred space.
Unchained, at peace, in divine embrace,
A harmonious world, a tranquil place.

CHAPTER 11
HERO UNCHAINED

Hero Unchained: Embracing the Balance of Divine Masculine and Feminine Energy

Imagine a world where heroism is defined not just by strength and courage but by the balance and integration of both divine masculine and feminine energies. Welcome to the realm of "Hero Unchained," where transcending traditional constraints allows us to embody a more complete and harmonious identity, merging assertiveness with empathy, structure with flexibility, and action with receptivity.

Healing the Wounded Feminine and Masculine

To achieve a balanced identity, it is crucial to address and heal the wounded aspects of both the feminine and masculine energies within us. This healing process involves recognizing and transforming limiting beliefs and patterns that hinder our growth.

Healing the Wounded Feminine

The wounded feminine may manifest as issues related to self-worth, receptivity, or emotional expression. Healing this aspect involves developing self-compassion, setting healthy boundaries, and embracing vulnerability. Techniques such as therapy, creative expression, and mindfulness can be particularly effective. For example, a woman dealing with issues of self-worth might engage in practices like affirmations and connect with supportive communities to reinforce her value and capabilities.

Healing the Wounded Masculine

The wounded masculine often presents excessive control, aggression, or difficulty in expressing emotions. Healing this aspect requires fostering emotional intelligence, embracing flexibility, and learning to balance assertiveness with empathy. Practices such as mindfulness, emotional intelligence training, and conflict resolution skills can support this healing process. For instance, a man struggling with aggression might use mindfulness techniques to manage his reactions and learn to express his emotions in a more balanced manner.

The Heroine's Journey: Integrating Archetypes for Healing

Maureen Murdock's "The Heroine's Journey" provides a valuable framework for understanding and integrating the archetypal patterns that influence our quest for balance and wholeness. Her model outlines a journey from external achievement to internal self-discovery and integration.

- **The Call to Adventure:** In the Heroine's Journey, the call to adventure symbolizes a challenge or awakening that prompts deeper self-exploration. This stage often involves confronting personal wounds and recognizing the need for healing. For example, a professional setback might trigger a deeper reflection on personal values and identity, encouraging an individual to embark on a journey of self-discovery.

- **The Descent into the Underworld:** This phase represents a journey into the unconscious, where individuals confront their shadows and wounded aspects. Engaging with archetypes such as the "Wounded Child" or "Victim" can help reveal these deep-seated patterns. For instance, exploring the "Wounded Child" archetype through self-reflection can illuminate unresolved issues and facilitate healing.

As a coach, I often help people navigate feelings of shame related to gender, sexuality, trauma, and desire. I remember a challenging time when I was working shifts and suffering from sleep deprivation, which led to unusual symptoms—a hormonal imbalance. I began noticing changes in my body, and my part-ner mentioned feeling a decrease in our intimacy and connec-tion. When I sought help, my doctor stood up, and yelled at me, shaming me. To make matters worse, the doctor documented a conversation that never took place, stating that extensive domes-tic violence was the cause—something we never discussed at all! I left feeling violated, traumatized, dirty, and impure.

This experience, combined with the abusive career counseling I had already endured, left me even more disconnected from my identity as a woman. While gender identity may only be one aspect of who we are, it's a vital part of our overall well-being. Survivors that I work with who've suffered sexual trauma are often re-traumatized by therapists, especially when it comes to feelings of shame, guilt, blame, and desire. Women have been historically shamed, persecuted, and cast out, while men often experience these issues differently. Reclaiming self-worth and embracing this part of identity is crucial to healing.

DANCING WITH A SHADOW NAMED DESIRE

In the twilight where whispers blend,
A shadow sways, both foe and friend,
Her name is Desire, a flickering flame,
A dance of longing, both wild and tame.

She beckons softly, with a sultry grace,
In the depths of night, I find her embrace,
A mirror reflecting what I hide away,
Secrets and yearnings, in disarray.

Her voice is a melody, sweet yet severe,
Echoing dreams that I hold most dear,
But in her rhythm, a fear does arise,
The cost of the dance, the weight of the ties.

With each turn, I teeter on the edge,
Tempted by beauty, I make my pledge,
To explore the depths where shadows play,
To face the darkness that won't fade away.

In the spotlight, we twirl and spin,
Her laughter lingers, a siren's din,
But in the hush, when the music fades,
I glimpse the truth in the masquerade.

Desire is a shadow, both dark and bright,
A reminder of dreams that ignite the night,
In this dance, I learn to embrace,
The light and the shadow, the fear, and the grace.

So I'll dance with her, through joy and despair,
With courage as my partner, and love in the air,
For in every shadow, there lies a chance,
To reclaim my power in this sacred dance.

The Rebirth and Integration: Rebirth involves integrating the lessons learned from the journey and emerging with a renewed sense of self. This phase often includes embracing both divine masculine and feminine energies in their balanced forms. For example, after navigating personal challenges, a woman might find empowerment by integrating her assertive and nurturing qualities, leading to a more harmonious and authentic self.

The Power of Integration

Integrating divine masculine and feminine energies is not about choosing one over the other but about finding a balance that enriches our lives. Drawing from ancient philosophies and symbols can further illustrate the significance of this integration.

- **Ancient Symbolism and Philosophy:** The Hindu deities Shiva and Shakti exemplify the union of divine masculine and feminine energies. Shiva represents consciousness and stability, while Shakti embodies dynamic energy and transformation. Their union symbolizes the potential for profound balance within everyone (Kumar, 2011). Similarly, the Yin–Yang symbol in Taoist tradition illustrates the interconnectedness of opposites, showing that true harmony arises from their dynamic interplay (Chan, 2010).

- **Harmonizing the Energies:** Achieving a balanced identity involves recognizing and harmonizing both divine masculine and feminine energies. This balance allows us to navigate challenges with strength and grace, making decisions that are informed by both logic and intuition. For instance, a leader who integrates both energies might approach challenges with a clear strategic vision (masculine) while remaining open to team feedback and emotional insights (feminine).

Navigating Imbalances

An imbalance between masculine and feminine energies can lead to various issues, including internal conflict and limited personal growth. Recognizing and addressing these imbalances is essential for achieving a more harmonious and fulfilling life.

- **Overemphasis on One Energy:** Overemphasizing one energy can lead to rigidity, control, or passivity. For example, excessive focus on the divine masculine may result in a domineering or aggressive approach, while an overemphasis on the divine feminine might lead to passivity or emotional overwhelm. Striking a balance between these energies helps avoid these extremes and fosters a more harmonious existence.

- **Internal Conflict and Disconnection:** Imbalances between these energies can cause internal conflict and feelings of disconnection. For instance, a person who struggles to reconcile assertiveness with sensitivity might experience frustration and confusion. Addressing these imbalances through self-reflection and integration practices can help restore equilibrium and enhance overall well-being.

Pathways to Balance

- **Self-Reflection and Journaling:** Regular self-reflection and journaling can help explore inner dynamics and identify areas of imbalance. Reflecting on experiences where one energy was dominant can provide insights into necessary adjustments. For instance, journaling about recent situations where assertiveness overshadowed empathy can reveal ways to achieve better balance.

- **Mindfulness and Meditation:** Mindfulness and meditation practices support the integration of divine energies. Visualizing a harmonious interplay between these energies can enhance self-awareness and emotional balance. Techniques such as guided visualizations can help individuals connect with and harmonize their inner masculine and feminine aspects.

- **Creative Expression:** Engaging in creative activities fosters divine feminine qualities such as intuition and receptivity. Creative expression provides a channel for exploring and integrating these energies, enriching personal growth and well-being. Activities like art, writing, or dance can help tap into intuitive and emotional depths, promoting balance and harmony.

The Journey of Hero Unchained

In the transformative journey of "Hero Unchained," true heroism is not about the dominance of one energy over another but about their seamless integration. Embracing both divine masculine and feminine energies allows us to achieve a balanced and authentic self, leading to a more fulfilling and empowered life. This journey invites us to break free from traditional constraints and celebrate the dynamic interplay of our inner energies, finding harmony in their integration.

Transcending the Glass

Imagine a glass surface where the divine masculine and feminine energies move, not as separate entities, but as fluid partners in a harmonious dance. This image captures the essence of how these energies can interact, merge, and transform when in balance. When envisioned together on the glass, the energies do not merely coexist; they perform a dynamic, synchronized dance that creates a beautiful, unified pattern.

ELYSIAN DREAM™

In the realm where dreams are spun,
Elysian fields await,
A world where men and women run,
To meet their destined fate.

A warrior's journey leads him there,
With courage as his guide,
His heart's desire, a love so rare,
In balance, they abide.

She, like diamonds' glimmering light,
A radiant soul, serene,
Together they dance through the night,
In a realm of evergreen.

Their union forms a sacred spell,
A bond of love and might,
In Elysian's peaceful dell,
They stand as one, united bright.

A hero's quest now intertwined,
With blissful moments shared,
Their spirits soar, both hearts aligned,
In love's pure grace ensnared.

Their strength lies not in force alone,
But in the power of the heart,
A balance found, the seed is sown,
For lives to never part.

In this tranquil, eternal place,
Where time's touch fades away,

Their love transforms, a sacred space,
Where souls in bliss will stay.

The journey's end, a new beginning,
As hearts entwine in song,
In Elysian's gentle spinning,
Their love will keep them strong.

A story etched in timeless stone,
Of peace and harmony,
The warrior and his love have grown,
In their divine journey.

The Dance of Balance

Visualizing the divine masculine and feminine energies dancing together on a glass surface offers a powerful metaphor for their potential to harmonize and elevate each other. This dance is not about the energies overpowering one another but about their mutual enhancement and synergy. The fluid, graceful movements on the glass illustrate how these energies can blend seamlessly, creating a more complete and balanced experience.

Flow and Flexibility

On the glass, the masculine energy might represent structured lines and shapes, symbolizing logic, direction, and discipline. The feminine energy, in contrast, might flow with curves and fluid patterns, embodying creativity, receptivity, and nurturing. Together, these movements create a fluid, dynamic interplay that highlights how structure and flexibility can complement each other, leading to a harmonious and vibrant whole.

Harmonious Interaction

The dance on the glass reflects the harmonious interaction between these energies. When the divine masculine and feminine move together, they create a pattern that is both intricate and balanced, illustrating how their integration can lead to a more profound and enriching experience. This visual representation emphasizes that the energies, while distinct, are interdependent and mutually reinforcing.

Experiencing the Dance

Experiencing the dance of divine energies on the glass involves embracing the dynamic interplay of structure and creativity in our lives. By integrating both energies, we can achieve a more harmonious and empowered state of being.

Balancing Action and Receptivity

Just as the masculine and feminine energies on the glass move together to create a unified pattern, balancing action and receptivity in our lives allows for a more comprehensive approach to challenges and opportunities. For example, setting clear goals (masculine) while remaining open to intuitive insights and feedback (feminine) leads to a more effective and fulfilling outcome.

Embracing Dualities

The dance on the glass represents the beauty of embracing dualities within us. By accepting and integrating both assertiveness and empathy, structure, and flexibility, we can navigate life with greater ease and grace. This integration fosters a deeper sense of self-awareness and authenticity, enriching our personal and professional experiences.

Cultivating the Dance

Cultivating the dance of divine energies involves intentional practices and mindset shifts that support their harmonious interaction.

Mindfulness and Reflection

Mindfulness practices help us become more aware of how divine energies are expressed in our lives. Reflecting on situations where one energy dominates over the other can provide insights into how to better balance them. For instance, noticing when assertiveness overshadows empathy can guide us in finding a more harmonious approach.

Creative Exploration

Engaging in creative activities allows us to explore and express both energies in their balanced forms. Artistic endeavors, such as painting or dance, can help integrate masculine structure with feminine flow, creating a balanced and expressive representation of our inner dynamics.

Symbolic Visualization

Visualization techniques can be used to imagine the dance of energies on the glass, creating a mental image of their harmonious interaction. Visualizing how these energies blend and interact can enhance our ability to integrate them into real-life situations, fostering a more balanced and empowered self.

The Art of Integration

The art of integration involves understanding that divine masculine and feminine energies are not opposing forces but complementary aspects of our being. When they dance together on the glass, they create a harmonious and dynamic pattern that reflects the richness of our inner world.

Celebrating Synergy

Recognizing and celebrating the synergy between these energies allows us to appreciate their unique contributions. Just as the dance on the glass creates a beautiful and unified pattern, integrating both energies in our lives leads to a more fulfilling and balanced experience.

Embracing the Whole Self

The dance of divine energies reminds us of the importance of embracing our whole selves. By integrating both masculine and feminine qualities, we can achieve a more comprehensive understanding of our identity and potential. This holistic approach fosters personal growth, creativity, and resilience.

The Journey of Harmonious Dance

In the journey of "Hero Unchained," the dance of divine masculine and feminine energies on the glass represents a powerful metaphor for balance and integration. By embracing the dynamic interplay of these energies, we can achieve a more harmonious and enriched experience, both within ourselves and in our interactions with the world. This dance invites us to celebrate the beauty of integration and to recognize the strength that comes from embracing all aspects of ourselves. It is a call to honor both action and reflection, courage and compassion, structure, and creativity.

As we move in rhythm with this sacred dance, we find peace in the union of our inner and outer worlds, realizing that true harmony arises not from denying any part of ourselves, but from weaving them together into a cohesive, radiant whole. In this balanced state, we transcend the limitations of our roles and step into our fullest potential, becoming the heroes and heroines of our own lives—unchained, authentic, and complete.

As we conclude the chapter on "Hero Unchained," we have explored how balancing the divine masculine and feminine energies allows us to break free from limiting roles and step into our full potential as integrated, authentic beings. This harmonious dance of energies teaches us that our true power lies in embracing every aspect of ourselves, creating a solid foundation for the next stage of our journey.

Now, we turn to a new challenge: understanding *The Veteran IDENTITY GAP*. Just as the unchained hero must navigate the delicate balance between inner strength and external roles, veterans face their own unique struggle in bridging the gap between their military and civilian identities. In the next chapter, we will delve into this transition, exploring the complexities, obstacles, and opportunities that come with redefining oneself after military service and how veterans can find alignment and purpose in their new civilian lives.

THE VETERAN IDENTITY

A soldier returns, weary and worn,
From battles fought where shadows were born.
He steps on familiar streets, yet they seem strange,
A world he once knew, now rearranged.

His eyes hold echoes of lands far away,
Where silence was pierced by the guns' loud array.
Now, there is a quiet, unsettling, and stark,
A void where once his heart held a spark.

He tries to blend with the passing crowd,
But the faces around seem lost in a shroud.
A smile exchanged, a nod, a brief word,
Yet his soul longs for what it once heard.

Memories haunt him, in the still of the night,
Of brothers in arms who vanished from sight.
He sees their faces in dreams, clear as day,
Their laughter, and tears, forever at bay.

The world rushes on, in its chaotic pace,
While he walks a path that is lost its grace.
The clock keeps ticking, yet he stands still,
A mind adrift, without a will.

The hero inside him whispers his name,
Urging him on, to find his new claim.
He seeks solace in the hearts of old friends,
Their voices a balm as the healing begins.

But the journey is long, and the struggle is real,
To mend a heart that needs time to heal.
The weight of his past, he carries like stone,
Yet he'll rise again, not facing this alone.

For though he may stumble, and though he may fall,
He'll learn to stand strong, to answer the call.
A new life awaits, with lessons hard-won,
A soldier at peace, as his journey's begun.

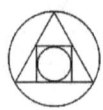

CHAPTER 12
THE VETERAN IDENTITY GAP

The Veteran IDENTITY GAP: Navigating the Transition to Civilian Life

Imagine standing at the edge of two worlds—the world you know intimately, where every day is filled with purpose, routine, and camaraderie, and a new world that seems uncertain, without the familiar guideposts. For many veterans, this is the reality of transitioning from military to civilian life. It is not just a change in scenery or daily routine; it's a profound shift in identity that can feel like a journey into the unknown.

The Hidden Challenges of Transition

Transitioning from military service to civilian life is one of the most significant identity shifts a person can experience. It is not just about finding a new job or adapting to a different environment; it's about redefining who you are in a world that no longer recognizes your rank, your achievements, or the skills you've honed over years of service. For many veterans, this transition can be fraught with unexpected challenges: feeling overqualified yet underemployed, losing the authority and respect that came with being a commander, and struggling to find a new professional identity. Research shows that up to 55% of our identity is shaped by our occupation, making this transition even more critical to navigate successfully.

Transitioning from military service to civilian life involves navigating an "IDENTITY GAP"—a disconnect between who veterans were in the military and who they need to become in the civilian sector. This gap can affect every aspect of a veteran's life, from their sense of self-worth to their mental health, relationships, and career. As a veteran embarking on this journey, understanding and addressing this IDENTITY GAP is crucial to creating a fulfilling post-military life.

1. **Loss of Structure and Routine:**

   The first thing many veterans notice when leaving the military is the sudden absence of structure. In the armed forces, your day is governed by a strict schedule and a clear chain of command. Every action, from the moment you wake up to when you go to sleep, is part of a larger purpose. This structure provides a sense of certainty and direction that is hard to replicate in civilian life. Without it, you might feel lost or overwhelmed by the sheer freedom of choice, which can lead to a loss of purpose. Studies show that veterans often struggle with the lack of a defined structure in civilian life, which can lead to difficulties in time management and contribute to a loss of identity (Journal of Clinical Psychology).

What Can You Do?

Embrace the flexibility of civilian life as an opportunity for growth. Begin by creating your own structure. Set daily goals, establish routines that align with your new aspirations, and be intentional about how you use your time. This will help recreate a sense of purpose and control.

2. **Redefining Identity and Purpose**

   In the military, your identity is often defined by your role, your rank, and your mission. Leaving that world behind can feel like losing a part of yourself. The question "Who am I without my uniform?" can be daunting, leading to a profound identity crisis. Research indicates that this loss of identity is one of the most significant psychological challenges veterans face during their transition, often resulting in feelings of isolation and depression.

What Can You Do?

Think of this period as a unique opportunity to explore new dimensions of yourself. Consider what aspects of your military identity you want to carry forward and which new aspects you want to develop. Engage in activities that align with your values and passions. Remember, your identity is not fixed; it is fluid and ever-evolving.

3. **Addressing Mental Health and Emotional Well-being**

   The psychological toll of military service, coupled with the stress of transition, can be significant. Veterans often experience mental health challenges, such as PTSD, anxiety, or depression. These conditions can worsen when transitioning to civilian life, particularly if there is a lack of understanding or support from the surrounding community. The Journal of Anxiety Disorders found that veterans are at a higher risk for mental health challenges during this time, with many experiencing symptoms of PTSD and depression.

What Can You Do?

Recognize the importance of mental health and seek support when needed. Engage with veteran support groups, counseling, or therapy to address these issues. It is crucial to remember that reaching out for help is a sign of strength, not weakness.

4. **Overcoming Social Isolation**

   The military fosters a deep sense of camaraderie and belonging. Many veterans leave service only to find themselves in a world where such bonds are rare. The loss of this social network can lead to feelings of loneliness and isolation, which in turn can make reintegration even more difficult.

What Can You Do?

Build new support networks by connecting with other veterans or groups that share your interests. Volunteering, joining community organizations, or engaging in new hobbies can help create a sense of belonging and purpose.

5. **Facing Employment Challenges**

Finding meaningful employment is often a major hurdle. You have unique skills—leadership, discipline, problem-solving—but translating these into a civilian context is not always straightforward. One of the most common experiences for veterans is finding themselves overqualified for the jobs available to them. The military provides a structured environment where every action, decision, and achievement has a direct impact. This often results in a highly specialized skill set that, in the civilian world, is sometimes overlooked or misunderstood by employers who do not know how to translate military experience into civilian roles.

For instance, a former military commander may have led teams in high-stress environments, managed complex projects, and made critical decisions with significant consequences. Yet, when they transition to the civilian workforce, they may find themselves in entry-level positions or roles that do not fully utilize their experience and skills. This misalignment can lead to a sense of underemployment and frustration, contributing to a deeper identity crisis.

The Institute for Veterans and Military Families reports that many veterans take jobs that do not fully utilize their skills, reinforcing feelings of inadequacy and widening the IDENTITY GAP.

6. **No Longer a Commander: The Impact on Professional Identity**

In the military, rank and role are clear indicators of status, authority, and respect. A commander, for example, holds significant power and influence, often making life-or-death decisions. The civilian workplace, however, does not operate with the same hierarchy or recognition of military accomplishments. Veterans may find themselves in positions where they no longer have the same authority or respect, leading to a profound loss of professional identity.

This shift from being a leader with a clear purpose to feeling like "just another employee" can be jarring. The sense of purpose and mission that came with military service is often replaced by a feeling of being adrift, unsure of where one fits in a civilian context. This can affect not only job satisfaction but also mental health and overall well-being.

How to Bridge the IDENTITY GAP: Finding Satisfaction in the Civilian Workforce

To bridge the IDENTITY GAP and find satisfaction in the civilian workforce, it is crucial to understand that this process is not just about finding a job—it is about redefining your identity and aligning your values, skills, and aspirations with a new environment. Here are strategies to help navigate this transition:

1. **Reframe Your Military Experience for Civilian Contexts:** Start by translating your military skills into language that civilian employers understand. Instead of listing military jargon on your resume, focus on the core competencies you have developed—leadership, project management, teamwork, decision-making, and adaptability. Consider using resources like veteran-specific job boards, resume workshops, or career coaching to better articulate your experience.

2. **Seek Roles that Value Your Skills:** Look for companies that recognize and value the unique skills veterans bring to the table. Many organizations have veteran hiring programs designed to match military skills with civilian roles. Networking with other veterans who have successfully transitioned can also provide valuable insights and opportunities.

3. **Build a New Community:** One of the most significant losses during the transition is the sense of camaraderie and community you had in the military. Seek out veteran sup-

port groups, professional organizations, or community activities that allow you to connect with others who understand your experiences. Building a new community can provide the social support necessary for a successful transition.

4. **Pursue Continuing Education or Certifications:** In some cases, veterans may need to pursue additional education or certifications to align their skills with civilian job requirements. This can also help bridge the gap between feeling overqualified and underemployed by expanding your qualifications and making you more competitive in the job market.

5. **Redefine Your Purpose:** While military service often provides a clear sense of mission and purpose, civilian life may not offer the same clarity. Take time to reflect on your values, strengths, and interests outside of the military context. What drives you? What kind of impact do you want to make in your civilian career? Redefining your purpose can help you find roles that are not only a good fit for your skills but also fulfilling and meaningful.

6. **Consider Counseling or Coaching:** Transitioning from a military to a civilian role can be emotionally and psychologically challenging. Seeking support from a professional counselor or career coach who specializes in working with veterans can provide guidance, coping strategies, and a safe space to process the emotional aspects of the transition.

Bridging the IDENTITY GAP

Navigating the IDENTITY GAP is about more than just surviving; it is about thriving in your new civilian life. Here are some practical steps to help you bridge that gap:

1. **Career Counseling and Mentorship:** Leverage career counseling to better understand how your military skills translate to civilian roles. Seek mentors who have successfully navigated the transition.

2. **Peer Support Programs:** Join veteran peer support programs to share experiences and build new identities in a supportive environment.

3. **Personal Development:** Engage in personal development programs that focus on self-awareness, emotional intelligence, and goal setting.

4. **Purpose and Meaning:** Reconnect with your values and identify new missions that resonate with your civilian life.

Embracing the Transformation

Transitioning from military to civilian life is not about letting go of your past but integrating it into your future. By addressing the IDENTITY GAP, you can find new purpose, build new relationships, and create a life that honors both your military and civilian selves. Remember, you have the power to shape your journey and transform challenges into opportunities for growth. As we close the chapter on "The Veteran IDENTITY GAP," we have uncovered the unique challenges veterans face when transitioning from military to civilian life. We explored the complexities of redefining one's identity, finding new purpose, and navigating the often-unseen obstacles that come with leaving behind a familiar world of service. Veterans must bridge the gap between who they were and who they are becoming, forging a path to a new sense of self.

Now, we move forward to examine *Inheritance*—a chapter that delves into the legacies we carry with us, both consciously and unconsciously. Whether shaped by our ancestry, culture, experiences, or choices, our inheritance plays a profound role in our identity. We will explore how understanding and embracing this inheritance can empower us to honor our past, shape our present, and create a future that aligns with our true selves. In doing so, we discover that our inheritance is not a burden to bear but a source of strength and wisdom that guides us on our journey.

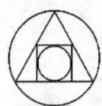

INHERITANCE

Passed through hands, from heart to heart,
A legacy of wounds that never part.
Shackled and bound, beaten by time,
Echoes of abuse in each generation's rhyme.

The shadow side of the mother wound,
Where dreams were buried, hope entombed.
In the darkness, Grief took root,
Her whispers cold, her touch acute.

But beneath the sorrow, a spark ignites,
A healing power, born of light.
The divine feminine calls her name,
To rise above, to break the chain.

Grief, once a shackle, now unfurls,
A banner of strength, a gift to the world.
For in her wounds, she finds her grace,
A sacred journey, a holy embrace.

From the shadows, she whispers again,
Her name is Grief—but she transcends the pain.
Healed by the power of the divine,
She claims her light, her soul's design.

CHAPTER 13
INHERITANCE

Healing the Hidden Wounds

Have you ever felt like something was holding you back, an invisible force that stops you from fully embracing who you are or achieving your true potential? These are the hidden wounds—those deep, unseen scars left by our past experiences with our family, our upbringing, and even our own lineage. The Father, Mother, Sister, and Womb wounds represent various aspects of our past that shape our identity, our relationships, and our sense of self. By understanding and healing these wounds, we can transform our lives, empower ourselves, and rewrite our story.

The Father Wound: Releasing the Fear of Inadequacy

The father wound arises from unmet needs or unresolved conflicts with the father figure in our lives. This wound may manifest as a constant feeling of not being good enough, a fear of failure, or even a resistance to authority. If you find yourself doubting your abilities, struggling with low self-esteem, or feeling unworthy of love and success, the father wound may play a role in your life. Healing this wound involves recognizing the impact of an absent, critical, or emotionally unavailable father and learning to rebuild your sense of self-worth and confidence.

Signs of the Father Wound:

- Feeling inadequate or unworthy.

- Struggling to trust or respect authority figures.

- Overwhelming fear of failure or need for perfectionism.

The Mother Wound: Embracing Self-Love and Nurturing

The mother wound often stems from emotional neglect or unmet needs from a mother figure. This can make it challenging to set healthy boundaries, practice self-care, or cultivate self-love. If you find yourself constantly putting others' needs before your own or repeating unhealthy patterns in relationships, the mother wound may be influencing your behavior. The path to healing involves learning to nurture yourself, set boundaries, and build a foundation of self-love and self-compassion.

Signs of the Mother Wound:

- Difficulty asserting personal needs or boundaries.

- Challenges with self-love and self-care.

- Tendency towards people-pleasing or emotional dependency.

The Sister Wound: Cultivating Connection and Collaboration

The sister wound reflects the scars of sibling rivalry, unresolved conflicts, or competition with female siblings. This wound often affects your ability to form supportive and trusting relationships with other women, creating feelings of jealousy, inadequacy, or betrayal. If you struggle to trust other women or feel threatened by their success, you may be experiencing the sister wound. Healing this wound requires recognizing these patterns and fostering a spirit of collaboration, trust, and genuine connection with other women.

Signs of the Sister Wound:

- Difficulty in maintaining supportive relationships with women.

- Feelings of jealousy, comparison, or inadequacy.

- Challenges in trusting or connecting with female friends or colleagues.

The Womb Wound: Reclaiming Creativity and Feminine Energy

The womb wound is deeply connected to our sense of creativity, femininity, and ancestral lineage. It encompasses unresolved traumas or issues related to birth, conception, or familial history. If you feel disconnected from your creativity, struggle with nurturing yourself or others, or feel a sense of disempowerment linked to your feminine identity, the womb wound may be impacting you. Healing this wound means reconnecting with your inner self, understanding your lineage, and embracing your inherent power and creativity.

Signs of the Womb Wound:

- Disconnection from creativity or difficulty nurturing oneself.

- Struggles with fertility, pregnancy, or feminine identity.

- A sense of disempowerment or lack of support from one's ancestry.

Inner Child Work: Reparenting Your Inner Self

Inner child work focuses on reconnecting with the part of yourself that still holds the pain of past wounds. This practice allows you to address unresolved childhood issues, nurture emotional needs, and develop self-compassion.

Exercises for Inner Child Work:

- **Write a Letter to Your Inner Child:** Reflect on your childhood experiences and write a letter to the child within you. Acknowledge their feelings, express love, and reassurance, and offer words of comfort. Revisit this letter often to reinforce positive self-talk and emotional healing.

- **Create a Safe Space:** Designate a space, either physically or mentally, where you can connect with your inner child. Use this space for self-reflection, creative expression, or activities that bring joy and safety.

Shadow Work: Embracing the Hidden Self

Shadow work involves exploring and integrating the hidden parts of yourself—those you may have suppressed or ignored. These hidden aspects can manifest as triggers, unconscious behaviors, or deep-seated fears. Through shadow work, you can achieve greater self-awareness and begin to transform these shadow aspects into sources of strength.

Exercises for Shadow Work:

- **Identify Your Triggers:** Notice emotional triggers and reactions that come up in daily life. Reflect on how these might relate to unresolved wounds or suppressed parts of yourself.

- **Journal Your Experiences:** Keep a journal of your experiences, noting any patterns, beliefs, or emotions that arise. Use this as a tool to explore and heal these hidden parts of yourself.

Attachment Styles: Understanding Relational Patterns

Understanding your attachment style is key to recognizing how early relationships with caregivers have shaped your current relational patterns and emotional responses. Whether secure, anxious, avoidant, or disorganized, each style offers insights into how unresolved wounds might be influencing your current relationships and self-perception.

Exercises to Explore Attachment Styles:

- **Identify Your Attachment Style:** Reflect on how you relate to others. Are you anxious, avoidant, or secure? Understanding this can provide valuable insights into your emotional landscape.

- **Seek Professional Guidance:** Consider therapy or counseling to help explore your attachment style and how it impacts your well-being and relationships.

Transforming Your Life Through Healing

Healing the father, mother, sister, and womb wounds is not a one-time event; it is a journey that requires courage, commitment, and self-compassion. By engaging in inner child work, shadow work, and understanding attachment styles, you can begin to heal these invisible scars and step into a more empowered, authentic version of yourself. Remember, your past does not define you—it informs you, guiding you toward a future where you can thrive, fully aligned with your true self.

Embrace this healing journey and step into your power. You have the strength to transform, heal, and create the life you truly desire!

As we conclude the chapter on INHERITANCE, we've explored the ways in which our past—our family histories, cultural legacies, and individual experiences—shapes our identities. We have seen how understanding and embracing this inheritance can empower us to build a life that honors our roots while also allowing us to evolve into who we truly wish to become. Our inheritance is a complex blend of gifts and challenges, each offering lessons that can guide us toward a more authentic self.

Now, we turn to a different kind of legacy: the emotional and societal inheritance that arises from profound cultural shifts.

In the chapter **Rosie's Grief**, we will delve into the transformation of women's roles during the women's rights movement and World War II—a period marked by both empowerment and profound loss. Through the lens of Rosie the Riveter, we will explore the grief of shifting identities, the unseen struggles, and the internal conflicts that emerge when societal expectations collide with personal aspirations. Here, we confront the complexities of what it means to be seen and unseen, to rise and to be held back, and to find our place in a world that is constantly redefining itself.

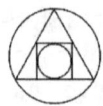

ROSIE'S GRIEF

Rosie stood, her sleeves rolled high,
A symbol strong, her spirit spry,
Yet in her heart, a quiet ache,
A grief that made her shoulders shake.

She fought for women to break free,
To lift each other, rise and see,
But in the shadows, whispers grew,
A subtle war that few folks knew.

Relational aggression, sharp and sly,
A dream grinch lurking, passing by,
With smiles that hid a hidden sting,
A silence where no bells would ring.

Not fists, but words that cut and bruise,
A cold exclusion, subtle ruse,
The gossip spread like poison vines,
To choke the dreams, to draw the lines.

Rosie's grief was deep and true,
For all the hearts it stole from view,
Women turned on women's hope,
Tangled tight in fear's own rope.

She saw them fight in muted cries,
With daggers hidden in their eyes,
A sisterhood betrayed by spite,
Turning day to endless night.

She mourned for what could truly be,
For bonds unbroken, wild and free,
For dreams that bloomed in open skies,
For hands held high, for lifted eyes.

Yet Rosie's grief, though dark and wide,
Was but a storm with waves that ride,
For she believed, in her strong way,
That every night becomes a day.

She called on all to break the chains,
To see beyond the narrow lanes,
To cast away the grinch's hold,
To find a strength both fierce and bold.

Rosie wept, but Rosie knew,
That grief could pave the way for new—
New chances, hope, and brighter dreams,
Where every voice together beams.

A future where the grief would cease,
Where women walk in their own peace,
Where dreams are safe from grinch's hand,
Where sisterhood reclaims the land.

CHAPTER 14
ROSIE'S GRIEF

Unmasking the Dream Grinches: How Relational Aggression is Sabotaging Sisterhoods

Imagine standing in a room filled with powerful women, each one shining like a star in her own right. You think, "This is what sisterhood looks like!" But beneath the surface, there is an invisible force at play—a force that causes some stars to dim while others burn brighter. This force is relational aggression, the hidden cost of women turning against each other. Are you aware of how it might be affecting you or those around you?

Understanding Relational Aggression: The Shadow that Blocks the Light

Relational aggression is like a Dream Grinch, quietly stealing joy, opportunity, and unity. It is a form of social manipulation where individuals, often unconsciously, undermine, exclude, or sabotage others through gossip, covert competition, or silent exclusion. While this behavior may seem small or insignificant, its impact is profound—creating a toxic environment that stifles creativity, trust, and growth.

What is Relational Aggression? Relational aggression is a type of social manipulation where individuals harm others through exclusion, gossip, or undermining. Relational aggression manifests as subtle or overt behaviors aimed at damaging someone else's social standing or sense of belonging. When relational aggression occurs among women, it can have significant negative effects on both their professional and personal identities.

It can take many forms:

- **Gossip:** Sharing rumors or confidential information to diminish someone's credibility.

- **Exclusion:** Deliberately leaving someone out of meetings, social gatherings, or projects.

- **Undermining:** Subtly discrediting someone's work, ideas, or character.

- **Passive-Aggressive Behaviors:** Smiling in public, criticizing in private, or withholding information and support.

How Relational Aggression Hurts Women

When women turn on each other, the damage is not just emotional or psychological—it is practical. It impacts careers, mental health, and the broader social fabric that women have fought so hard to weave. Relational aggression keeps women from rising together, creating barriers that are often invisible but very real.

- **Loss of Confidence:** Women who experience relational aggression may start to doubt their own abilities and worth, leading to decreased self-esteem and increased anxiety.

- **Impaired Collaboration:** A culture of mistrust makes it difficult to work together effectively, stifling innovation and creativity.

- **Diminished Opportunities:** When women do not support each other, they miss opportunities for mentorship, sponsorship, and professional growth.

- **Reinforced Stereotypes:** Relational aggression perpetuates harmful stereotypes that women are too emotional or competitive to lead effectively.

How Relational Aggression Affects Women's Identity

1. **Erosion of Self-Esteem and Self-Worth**

   ▪ **Impact on Personal Identity:** Relational aggression can undermine a woman's sense of self by targeting her social standing, self-esteem, and emotional well-being. When women experience exclusion or manipulation from their peers, they may start to internalize negative feelings, doubting their value and self-worth.

   ▪ **Impact on Professional Identity:** In professional settings, relational aggression often involves subtle forms of undermining, such as spreading rumors, withholding information, or ostracizing colleagues. This behavior can lead to a decrease in confidence and the ability to assert oneself in the workplace, affecting one's career trajectory and professional reputation.

2. **Disruption of Social Belonging**

   ▪ **Impact on Personal Identity:** Humans are inherently social creatures, and feeling excluded or targeted disrupts a sense of belonging. For women, relational aggression can lead to feelings of isolation and a diminished sense of community, which are critical components of a healthy personal identity.

   ▪ **Impact on Professional Identity:** Professional environments often rely on networking, collaboration, and mentorship. Relational aggression can inhibit these connections, preventing women from forming strong professional networks and support systems, which are vital for career advancement and professional growth.

3. **Inhibition of Leadership and Advancement Opportunities**

   ▪ **Impact on Professional Identity:** Relational aggression can prevent women from assuming leadership roles or advancing in their careers. For example, women may be labeled as "difficult" or "not a team player" due to relational aggression, which can reduce their chances of receiving promotions, leadership opportunities, or professional development.

- **Impact on Personal Identity:** When women are blocked from leadership roles or advancement, they may experience a sense of loss or frustration with their career identity. This can further impact how they view themselves and their capabilities.

4. **Reinforcement of Stereotypes and Gender Norms**

- **Impact on Professional Identity:** Relational aggression among women can perpetuate harmful stereotypes, such as the notion that women are "catty" or "emotional" in the workplace. These stereotypes can further marginalize women and limit their opportunities for growth.

- **Impact on Personal Identity:** These dynamics can cause women to conform to stereotypical gender roles to avoid conflict or aggression, limiting their personal expression and development.

5. **Creation of a Hostile Work Environment**

- **Impact on Professional Identity:** A work culture where relational aggression is prevalent can be toxic, leading to decreased job satisfaction, burnout, and turnover. Women may feel less motivated to engage fully with their work or contribute innovative ideas, which can stifle their professional identity development.

- **Impact on Personal Identity:** Over time, a hostile work environment can cause women to disengage from their authentic selves, adopting survival tactics such as self-censorship or people-pleasing, which can erode their personal identity.

6. Damage to Mental Health and Well-Being

- **Impact on Personal and Professional Identity:** Experiencing relational aggression can lead to anxiety, depression, and stress, which can affect all facets of a woman's identity. Poor mental health can impact decision-making, creativity, and performance in the workplace, further hindering career progression and self-perception.

- Relational aggression not only harms individual women but also undermines the collective progress of women in society. Recognizing and addressing these behaviors can empower women to build healthier, more supportive environments that foster growth and positive identity development.

Recognizing Relational Aggression in Others

To overcome relational aggression, we must first recognize it.

Look for these signs in your workplace or social environment:

- **The Fake Friend:** Someone who pretends to support you but subtly undermines you behind your back.

- **The Gatekeeper:** A person who controls access to information, opportunities, or networks and uses this control to exclude others.

- **The Invisible Leader:** A woman in power who does not mentor, promote, or visibly support other women.

By becoming aware of these behaviors, we can begin to dismantle the invisible barriers they create.

The Hidden Wound: How Relational Aggression Impacts Women's Progress

Rosie the Riveter, the symbol of female empowerment, would feel a deep sadness to see how these invisible battles are fought. Instead of unity and strength, there is division and competition.

When women turn against each other, it does more than hurt feelings—it contributes to systemic inequality.

Women who face relational aggression may experience social isolation, loss of career opportunities, and even financial instability. The emotional toll can lead to mental health challenges such as anxiety, depression, and burnout. Relational aggression is not just a personal issue; it is a public one that impacts entire communities and economies.

> *"There's a special place in hell for women who don't help each other." – **Madeleine Albright***

Why Does It Happen? The Shift to Masculine Aggression

The entrance of women into male-dominated workplaces brought new challenges and pressures. Traits like competition, assertiveness, and aggression—historically, associated with men— began to infiltrate how women interacted. For some, these traits became tools for survival, even if it meant tearing down others in the process.

This shift led to a distorted feminine identity, where collaboration, empathy, and nurturing were overshadowed by tactics designed to 'win' in environments that rewarded such behaviors. While it may have seemed like the only way to succeed, it has often come at the cost of authentic connection and mutual support among women.

The Mask of False Collaboration

There is a pervasive narrative in today's world: women supporting women, promoting abundance, and working together for greater success. Yet, many women feel that this narrative is just a mask—something worn to appear supportive while secretly undermining others.

The "mask" of false collaboration is especially damaging in leadership roles, where women have the power to make or break each other's careers. When women in leadership fail to genuinely support their peers, the cost is felt across all levels—creating a ripple effect that keeps women from reaching their full potential.

The High Price of Exclusion

When women do not help each other establish a professional identity, it is more than just a lost opportunity—it's an act of exclusion that denies others a sense of belonging and purpose. This exclusion steals not just identities but dreams, hopes, and futures. The wound of feeling invisible can cut deeper than any other— leading to long-lasting impacts on mental health, self-worth, and professional growth.

Leadership Failure: The Cost of Betrayal

Women in leadership have a unique opportunity and responsibility to pave the way for those who follow. When they fail to do so—when they exploit their position to further their own ambitions while holding others back—they perpetuate a cycle of inequality and isolation.

For those of us who have felt the sting of such betrayal, the impact is deeply personal. We know what it feels like to be on the outside, looking in—to feel invisible, discarded, or even betrayed by those who should be allies.

A Call to Rise: The New Vision of Rosie

What would a modern Rosie look like today? She would be someone who recognizes the value of genuine support and mentorship—someone who lifts others as she climbs. This Rosie understands that her success is tied to the success of other women. She sees other women not as competitors, but as allies in the fight for equality, justice, and shared achievement.

A New Legacy of Solidarity

The grief of Rosie is not just about the past—it is about the choices we make today. Will we continue to hide behind masks, or will we take them off and truly support one another? The choice is ours, and it is one that will define the future for generations to come. Let's choose to build a world where women are not just surviving but thriving together.

Narcissistic individuals often use relational aggression to assert control, maintain status, and enhance their self-image. Relational aggression includes behaviors such as gossiping, exclusion, backstabbing, and other forms of social manipulation that harm others indirectly. Narcissists may engage in these behaviors to reinforce their sense of superiority, protect their fragile self-esteem, and punish those they perceive as threats to their ego or status.

Relationship Between Relational Aggression and Narcissism

1. **Narcissistic Traits and Relational Aggression:** Individuals with narcissistic traits, such as a grandiose sense of self-importance, a need for admiration, and a lack of empathy, are more likely to engage in relational aggression. These behaviors are used to maintain their social status, protect their self-image, and control how others perceive them.

   Research has shown that narcissistic individuals often engage in manipulative behaviors to control relationships and assert dominance, which aligns closely with relational aggression.

2. **Relational Aggression as a Tool for Social Status and Control:** Narcissists often perceive relationships in terms of power dynamics and may use relational aggression to manipulate social hierarchies to their advantage. By undermining others through gossip, exclusion, or other indirect forms of aggression, they aim to weaken potential competitors and ensure their own position of authority and influence.

3. **Fragile Self-Esteem and Relational Aggression:** Narcissists often have fragile self-esteem despite their outward

confidence. They may resort to relational aggression to defend against perceived slights or challenges to their self-image. When they feel threatened, they may engage in social manipulation to discredit or isolate others who are perceived as a threat.

4. **Lack of Empathy and Increased Aggressive Behaviors:** Narcissists display a lack of empathy, which allows them to engage in aggressive behaviors without regard for the emotional impact on others. This lack of empathy facilitates their use of relational aggression as they may not fully comprehend or care about the harm they cause to others' reputations or well-being.

5. **Reinforcement of Narcissistic Supply:** Relational aggression may also be used by narcissists to secure a "narcissistic supply," which is a continuous need for attention, validation, and admiration from others. By manipulating relationships and creating drama or conflict, narcissists can position themselves at the center of attention, satisfying their need for admiration and control.

Relational aggression is closely tied to narcissism, as it serves the narcissist's need for control, status, and validation while simultaneously undermining the social and professional standing of those around them. Recognizing this link is essential for understanding the dynamics of relational aggression in various contexts.

Narcissism and Identity are deeply intertwined, as narcissism fundamentally affects how individuals construct, perceive, and maintain their sense of self. For narcissists, identity is often shaped by a combination of grandiosity, fragile self-esteem, and a constant need for external validation. This results in an unstable and inflated self-concept that requires continuous reinforcement through external sources like admiration, status, and control over others.

How Narcissism Affects Identity

1. **Grandiose Self-Concept:** Narcissists typically have an inflated or grandiose self-concept, viewing themselves as special, unique, or superior to others. This self-concept is often built on a fragile foundation that is vulnerable to criticism or failure. To maintain this inflated self-view, narcissists may overemphasize their achievements, talents, or importance and seek out situations that validate this self-concept.

2. **Dependence on External Validation:** A narcissist's identity is highly dependent on external validation. They require constant admiration and attention from others to sustain their self-esteem. Without this "narcissistic supply," they may feel empty, worthless, or insignificant. This reliance on others' approval makes their identity unstable, as it can fluctuate based on external feedback and social status.

3. **Lack of True Self-Understanding:** Narcissists often lack a stable, internal sense of self. Their identity is not rooted in a genuine understanding of who they are but is instead constructed around external achievements, appearance, or social status. This makes their sense of self shallow and dependent on maintaining a certain image or facade.

4. **Fragile Self-Esteem and Defensive Mechanisms:** Despite their outward confidence, narcissists usually have fragile self-esteem. They may use defensive mechanisms like denial, projection, or rationalization to protect their self-image from perceived threats. Any criticism or perceived slight can trigger feelings of shame or inadequacy, leading to aggressive or defensive behaviors.

5. **Identity Diffusion and Role Confusion:** Narcissistic individuals may experience identity diffusion, where they struggle to integrate various aspects of their personality into a cohesive whole. This can lead to role confusion and difficulty in maintaining consistent relationships or professional roles. They may shift between different personas or identities depending on the situation, often to maintain control or receive admiration.

6. **Manipulation of Identity in Relationships:** Narcissists often manipulate their own and others' identities in relationships. They may adopt personas that they believe will attract admiration or manipulate others into roles that serve their need for control and validation. This can lead to a lack of authentic connections and relationships built on manipulation rather than mutual respect and understanding.

7. **Fear of Authenticity and Vulnerability:** Narcissists may fear authenticity and vulnerability because these states could expose their flaws or inadequacies. Instead, they construct an idealized version of themselves to present to the world, which prevents them from genuinely knowing themselves or forming authentic relationships. This fear of vulnerability further prevents self-growth and self-awareness, contributing to their identity's instability.

Impact of Narcissism on Professional and Social Identity

1. **Professional Identity:** Narcissists may define their professional identity through achievements, titles, or positions that confer status and authority. They often seek leadership roles not to serve others but to gain admiration and control. This drive for recognition can lead to unethical behavior, manipulation, or sabotage of colleagues to maintain their perceived status. Their sense of worth is often tied to their professional identity, making them extremely sensitive to criticism or perceived threats in the workplace.

2. **Social Identity:** Socially, narcissists often curate a public persona that portrays them as successful, charming, and accomplished. They may use social connections to enhance their status or influence, often focusing on relationships that provide them with social benefits. However, their relationships may lack depth and authenticity, as they are primarily based on the narcissist's needs rather than genuine connection or empathy.

3. **Challenges in Identity Development:** Narcissistic traits can interfere with healthy identity development. Because narcissists often lack self-awareness and are driven by a need for validation, they may struggle with introspection, self-reflection, and self-improvement. This can hinder their ability to develop a well-rounded, integrated identity that includes both strengths and weaknesses.

Narcissism profoundly affects how individuals construct, maintain, and perceive their identities, often leading to a fragile, externally validated, and manipulated sense of self that can result in both personal and professional difficulties.

Identity diffusion and role confusion in narcissists can manifest in several ways, both at home and in professional settings. Here are some examples:

At Home

1. **Inconsistent Parenting Style:** A narcissistic parent may alternate between being overly indulgent and excessively controlling with their children, causing confusion about their role as a caregiver.

2. **Emotional Manipulation:** They may struggle to maintain consistent emotional boundaries, swinging between overly affectionate displays and cold detachment, leaving family members uncertain about their relationship dynamics.

3. **Constant Need for Validation:** A narcissist may shift between different personas or roles to gain admiration or attention from family members, showing confusion about who they truly are or what they value.

4. **Unstable Relationships:** Frequent changes in their relationships, such as cycles of idealization and devaluation of their partner, can demonstrate confusion about what they want or need from a relationship.

5. **Lack of Authenticity:** A narcissist may mimic or copy family members' hobbies, interests, or behaviors to feel relevant or admired, showing a lack of a solid self-concept.

At Work

1. **Frequent Job Changes:** They might change jobs or career paths frequently due to conflicts with colleagues or a perceived lack of recognition, indicating confusion about their professional identity or goals.

2. **Inconsistent Leadership Style:** A narcissistic leader may alternate between micromanaging and being hands-off, creating confusion among their team about expectations and direction.

3. **Taking Credit for Others' Work:** To feed their need for recognition, a narcissist might claim ownership of others' ideas or projects, displaying a lack of clear professional identity or role boundaries.

4. **Conflict with Authority:** They may have trouble respecting authority figures or aligning with company culture, frequently challenging superiors and struggling to fit into a defined role.

5. **Manipulating Coworkers:** Engaging in gossip, backstabbing, or creating workplace factions to maintain control or appear dominant, showing a lack of clarity in their own professional role and ethics.

In Business

1. **Lack of Clear Vision:** A narcissistic entrepreneur or business leader may frequently change business strategies or goals based on whims or external validation rather than a consistent mission or vision.

2. **Role Swapping:** They might oscillate between being the "visionary leader" and the "hands-on manager," leaving employees and partners confused about their actual roles and responsibilities.

3. **Imposter Syndrome Masked by Overconfidence:** They may project extreme confidence publicly while privately

doubting their abilities or needing constant reassurance, indicating a lack of solid identity.

4. **Unstable Alliances**: Quickly forming and dissolving business partnerships, reflecting confusion about trust, loyalty, and their business identity.

5. **Fluctuating Ethical Standards**: Their moral compass may change depending on who they need to impress or the immediate benefit, showing inconsistency in values and principles.

As we reflect on "Rosie's Grief," we have journeyed through the complexities of women's evolving roles during the women's rights movement and World War II. We have seen how the iconic figure of Rosie the Riveter symbolizes both empowerment and the unseen sorrow of shifting identities. The grief of being caught between expectations and aspirations, the pain of relational aggression, and the struggle for visibility have all underscored the deep, emotional wounds women can carry.

Now, we turn to *Rosie's Wisdom*, where we explore the path to healing and transformation. Here, we will uncover how women can empower one another, moving beyond competition, envy, and insecurity. This chapter will delve into how we can foster true collaboration, build each other up, and create a legacy of strength and unity. In Rosie's Wisdom, we find the courage to rewrite the narrative—not just for ourselves but for future generations of women who will rise, supported and seen.

ROSIE THE RIVETER: A HEROINE'S ANTHEM

With rolled-up sleeves and calloused hands,
She forged her place in unknown lands,
A factory floor, a steel domain,
Where every rivet bore her name.

Rosie stood tall beneath the grime,
Her spirit fierce, her heart in rhyme.
She broke the mold they cast for her,
A barrier breaker, a barrier blur.

The glass above was thick and cold,
A ceiling built from ages old,
But Rosie swung her hammer high,
And dared to question, dared to try.

She shattered norms with every blow,
Made space for dreams to seed and grow.
Her voice a song, her stance a fight,
A heroine dancing in the light.

Yet, Rosie's strength was not her own,
But rooted deep in seeds once sown
By every woman, side by side,
Who shared the load, who matched her stride.

A sisterhood that knew no end,
From battle scars, their hearts did mend.
They raised each other, hands entwined,
Empowered, free, with strength combined.

Not just for war, nor man's applause,
But for the right to shape their cause.
To work, to lead, to love, to learn,
True women's power—rightly earned.

For Rosie knew, as all women must,
That freedom blooms from more than trust.
It's in the courage to be true,
To lift as one, to break through.

So here's to Rosie, and every name,
Whoever dared to play the game,
Who saw the ceiling, and thought—"Not I,"
Who spread her wings and learned to fly.

She's every woman, fierce and bright,
A heroine who knows her might.
In every heart, her spirit's flame,
A light that breaks through glass and shame.

CHAPTER 15
ROSIE'S WISDOM

Empowering Women

In a world that often pits women against each other, how do we turn envy into empowerment and competition into collaboration? Let's learn from Rosie's wisdom and unlock the true power of sisterhood!

Overcoming Envy and Insecurity

Envy can be one of the most destructive forces in any relationship, particularly among women. It often manifests as resentment toward another woman's success, beauty, or opportunities and is usually rooted in deep-seated insecurity. This insecurity makes us feel that we are not enough and that someone else's achievements somehow diminish our own worth.

The first step in overcoming envy is to confront our insecurities head-on. Ask yourself: Why do I feel threatened by another woman's success? What insecurities are driving this envy? Engage in deep and honest self-reflection, no matter how uncomfortable it may feel. Only by acknowledging these feelings can we begin to dismantle the internal barriers that prevent us from celebrating one another's achievements.

Gratitude is another powerful antidote to envy. By focusing on our own unique strengths and accomplishments, we shift our attention away from comparison and towards appreciation. Start a daily practice of writing down three things you are grateful for—especially qualities, skills, or opportunities unique to you. Gratitude turns competition into collaboration; instead of seeing another woman's success as a threat, view it as an inspiration, a beacon that if she can achieve greatness, so can you.

When women feel secure in themselves, they are far more likely to support each other in bridging IDENTITY GAPs. This support is transformative—it empowers women to navigate life transitions, career changes, or personal crises with confidence and resilience, knowing they are not alone.

To overcome envy, it is essential to confront our insecurities head-on. Engage in a process of self-reflection to answer these shadow work journaling questions:

1. What specific qualities or achievements in others trigger feelings of envy for me?

2. How does my envy make me feel about myself?

3. What insecurities are underlying these feelings of envy?

4. How can I address these insecurities directly to improve my self-worth?

Another effective antidote to envy is gratitude. By focusing on our strengths and accomplishments, we shift from comparison to appreciation. Start a daily gratitude practice, noting:

1. Three things I am grateful for today.

2. Unique qualities and achievements that I bring to the table.

3. Instances where I have overcome challenges and succeeded.

Building Confidence and Self-Esteem

At the core of true empowerment is confidence. Yet many women struggle with self-esteem issues that undermine their ability to uplift one another. When we feel inadequate, we may attempt to compensate by undermining others or refusing to share knowledge, hoarding resources, and fearing being overshadowed. These behaviors only perpetuate cycles of disempowerment.

To build confidence, begin with self-acceptance. Recognize your own strengths and weaknesses without judgment or comparison. Understand that confidence is not a finite resource—it grows with practice and reinforcement. Take on new challenges, seek out new experiences, and celebrate your victories, no matter how small. This growth mindset will help you build the self-assurance needed to empower yourself and others.

Mentorship is a critical component in building confidence. Women in leadership positions have a unique opportunity to mentor their peers, passing on valuable knowledge, skills, and a sense of worth. When you mentor another woman, you create a ripple effect: as she gains confidence, she is better positioned to lift others up, creating a powerful cycle of empowerment.

Confidence is especially vital when it comes to bridging IDENTITY GAPs. Women who are secure in their own identities can offer invaluable insights, encouragement, and resources to those navigating their own paths of self-discovery and transformation.

Building Confidence and Self-Esteem

To build confidence, begin with self-acceptance. Reflect on these shadow work journaling questions:

1. What are my core strengths and weaknesses?

2. How do I currently perceive my own value and abilities?

3. What past experiences have shaped my self-esteem, both positively and negatively?

4. How can I reframe my past failures or perceived shortcomings as learning opportunities?

Confidence grows through practice and reinforcement. Embrace new challenges, celebrate small victories, and seek mentorship. Women in leadership can offer guidance that reinforces a sense of worth, creating a ripple effect of confidence and empowerment.

Moving Beyond Competition: A New Paradigm of Success

For too long, women have been conditioned to view success through a competitive lens. This mindset is reinforced by societal structures that reward individual achievement over collective progress. But what if we redefined success? Imagine a world where women do not climb the ladder alone, but build ladders for one another, knowing that true success is not measured by how high we climb, but by how many we bring along with us.

Shifting from competition to collaboration requires challenging the scarcity mindset—the belief that opportunities for success are limited. Embrace the concept of abundance: there is enough success to go around. When women see each other as allies, they are more likely to support one another's endeavors and share resources generously.

This new paradigm also celebrates diverse paths to achievement. Success is not a one-size-fits-all concept, and it shouldn't be. Recognize and honor the diverse ways women can contribute—through leadership, creativity, caregiving, innovation, and more. When we value each other's unique contributions, we move beyond the narrow definitions of success that often drive competition and conflict.

By supporting each other's unique paths, we create an environment where everyone has the chance to define and achieve success on their own terms. This environment is crucial for helping women bridge their IDENTITY GAPs, whether they are transitioning to a new career, navigating a life change, or exploring new aspects of themselves.

To shift from competition to collaboration, challenge the scarcity mindset and embrace abundance. Reflect on these journaling prompts:

1. How has competition shaped my view of success?

2. In what ways have I seen collaboration lead to greater collective success?

3. How can I shift my focus from individual achievement to supporting the success of others?

4. What steps can I take to build a network of support rather than rivalry?

Celebrate diverse paths to achievement and recognize the diverse ways women can contribute. Success should be valued in all its forms—leadership, creativity, caregiving, and innovation.

Rosie's Blueprint: Empowerment Through Authenticity

So, what would Rosie's wisdom look like in practice? An empowered woman, according to Rosie's blueprint, embodies authenticity in every aspect of her life. She understands that true empowerment is not about pretending to support others; it's about genuinely investing in their success. This woman is secure in her own worth, free from the need to compare herself to others. She celebrates her peers' achievements, knowing that another woman's success does not diminish her own.

Rosie's empowered woman is a champion of collaboration. She knows that collective success is more valuable than individual accolades. Instead of hoarding knowledge or resources, she shares them generously, understanding that by helping others rise, she elevates herself, too. She approaches every interaction with authenticity, fostering genuine connections based on mutual respect and trust.

This empowered woman is also a mentor and advocate. She uses her position to lift those who are just starting out, offering guidance, support, and encouragement. She challenges the status quo, refusing to play by the rules of a system that pits women against each other. Instead, she creates new rules—ones that prioritize collaboration, empathy, and shared success.

Most importantly, Rosie's empowered woman actively works to bridge the IDENTITY GAPs that many women face. She recognizes that identity is not static; it evolves over time. She supports other women in their journeys of self-discovery and growth. Through mentorship, advocacy, or simply being a role model, she helps others navigate the complexities of defining and redefining their identities in an ever-changing world.

To embody Rosie's empowered woman, consider these shadow work journaling questions:

1. How authentic am I in my interactions with others?

2. What fears or insecurities might be influencing my behavior towards other women?

3. How can I move from superficial support to genuine collaboration?

4. In what ways can I actively support other women in their personal and professional growth?

This empowered woman champions mentorship and advocacy. She creates new rules—prioritizing collaboration, empathy, and collective success—and actively works to bridge IDENTITY GAPs.

Conclusion: Embracing Rosie's Wisdom for a Brighter Future

Rosie's wisdom is a powerful call to action. By moving beyond superficial displays of support and fostering a culture of genuine empowerment, we can create a world where women truly uplift each other. Confronting insecurities, building confidence, and redefining success are crucial steps in this transformative journey. Let's embrace Rosie's wisdom and commit to a future where every woman can thrive and contribute to the collective success of all.

Having explored "Rosie's Wisdom," we have seen how the power of collaboration, support, and genuine connection can heal the invisible wounds women often carry. We have witnessed the transformation that occurs when we choose to uplift one another, breaking the cycles of envy and insecurity to build a foundation of empowerment and solidarity.

Now, we journey deeper into the **Dark Night of the Soul**, where we confront the inner landscapes that shape our most profound transformations. This chapter will explore the moments of deep despair and intense struggle that tests our strength and reveal the depths of our resilience. Here, in the shadows, we find the opportunity for growth, awakening, and the discovery of our true selves—illuminating a path forward from darkness into light.

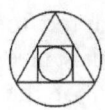

CHAPTER 16
DARK NIGHT OF THE SOUL

Navigating the Dark Night of the Soul: A Journey Through Identity, Transformation, and Resolution

Picture yourself standing on the edge of an immense abyss, a chasm of profound depth and darkness stretching out before you. The path forward is obscure, and the very ground beneath your feet seems to crumble away. This daunting scenario embodies the "Dark Night of the Soul"—a profound, often disorienting phase where your old identity dissolves, making way for a more authentic and empowered self. Understanding and navigating this process can illuminate the path to personal transformation and renewal.

Confronting the Abyss: Understanding the Dark Night of the Soul

The "Dark Night of the Soul," a term introduced by the 16th-century mystic Saint John of the Cross, represents a period of intense spiritual and psychological crisis. It signifies a deep inner turmoil where old structures and identities collapse, leaving one in a state of existential confusion and despair. Originally used in a spiritual context, this concept has been adapted to describe profound psychological crises where individuals face intense personal and emotional challenges (Saint John of the Cross, 1585).

In modern psychology, the Dark Night is closely related to Carl Jung's concept of the shadow. Jung proposed that the shadow encompasses the parts of ourselves that are often repressed or denied, revealing deep-seated fears and unresolved conflicts (Jung, 1953). This period of confronting the shadow is essential for personal growth, as it pushes us to face aspects of ourselves we might otherwise avoid. This crisis is also a crucial time to face the fairytales, or myths of the collective unconscious.

Carl Jung's Archetypes: Navigating the Self, Persona, Shadow, and Anima/Animus

To navigate the Dark Night of the Soul, it is essential to understand Carl Jung's key archetypes: the Self, Persona, Shadow, and Anima/Animus. These elements provide a framework for understanding the complexities of the human psyche and the transformative journey through the Dark Night.

1. **The Self:** The Self represents the totality of the psyche, encompassing both conscious and unconscious aspects. It is the core of one's being, the true essence that lies beyond social roles and external identities. Jung saw the Self as the goal of individuation, the process of integrating all parts of the psyche into a harmonious whole (Jung, 1953). Integration into a whole is a return to paradise.

2. **The Persona:** The Persona is the mask or social identity we present to the world. It is the adaptive aspect of ourselves shaped by societal expectations, norms, and roles. While necessary for navigating daily life, over-identification with the Persona can lead to a disconnection from the deeper aspects of the Self (Jung, 1953). During the Dark Night, the Persona often dissolves, revealing the authentic Self beneath.

3. **The Shadow:** The Shadow comprises the parts of ourselves that we reject, repress, or deny. It includes both positive and negative aspects that do not align with our conscious self-image. Confronting the Shadow during the Dark Night involves facing fears, insecurities, and unresolved conflicts that have been buried in the unconscious. This process is crucial for growth, as it allows for the integration of previously disowned aspects, leading to a more authentic and complete sense of self (Jung, 1953).

4. **The Anima/Animus:** The Anima (feminine aspect in men) and Animus (masculine aspect in women) represent the unconscious feminine and masculine qualities within each person. These archetypes influence our relationships, emotions, and inner balance. The Dark Night often involves reconciling these aspects to achieve psychological wholeness, fostering a deeper connection with oneself and others (Jung, 1953).

Descent into Chaos

The journey through the Dark Night begins with an awakening to a profound sense of loss or disillusionment. This stage is marked by a descent into darkness, a departure from familiar beliefs, goals, or identities, much like the hero's journey's "Threshold Crossing," where one ventures into unknown territory, leaving behind the security of the known (Campbell, 1949). This descent parallels the mythological River Lethe that borders Elysium, a river in the underworld that induces forgetfulness. Here, the challenge is to remember who you truly are amid the chaos.

Exercise: Embracing the Unknown

▪ Write about a significant loss or change you have experienced. Reflect on how this loss has challenged your identity and what emotions are surfacing.

▪ Create a vision board that visually represents your hopes and fears during this transition. Use this board as a tool to help guide you through uncertainty.

"The world will ask you who you are, and if you don't know, the world will tell you." -CARL JUNG

Shadow Factory

As you delve deeper into the darkness, you confront the shadow aspects of yourself. This stage involves intense introspection, where you face fears and insecurities that have long been suppressed. Engaging with these aspects is crucial for personal healing and transformation.

The alchemical **Elysian Dream™ Philosopher's Stone** embodies the ideals of love, strength, courage, healing, truth, the union of opposites, a return to paradise, and living a valuable life. Represented as an elemental diamond—a symbol of ultimate transformation—it serves as a portal to one's own liminal world, the space where chaos and creation meet. Rooted in ancient myth, diamonds were believed to be the "Rock of the Gods," powerful stones containing divine essence. This sacred elixir of transformation enables the journey to self-discovery and empowerment, encouraging connection with both one's inner and higher self.

In Jungian psychology, symbols like the diamond and mandala reflect the journey to wholeness or individuation, the process of realizing one's unique potential. The mandala, which means "circle" in Sanskrit, represents the integrated self—a balanced unity of conscious and unconscious. According to Jung, mandalas often emerge in times of significant personal change or healing, appearing in dreams or art to signify inner transformation. In many cultures, they symbolize harmony, providing a space for reflection, healing, and creative insight.

Together, the **Elysian Dream™ Philosopher's Stone** and the mandala offer transformative pathways, bridging the conscious and unconscious and uniting us with the divine, the self, and the boundless potential for creativity and growth.

Exercise: Shadow Work Journal

- Identify recent triggers that have provoked strong emotional reactions. Journal about these experiences and explore what they reveal about your inner fears or unresolved issues.

- Engage in a dialogue with your shadow self. Write out a conversation between your conscious self and these hidden aspects. This exercise can help you understand and integrate these parts of your identity.

- What masks do you wear?

- What aspects of Anima /Animus do you embody?

The Crucible of Transformation

In this phase, the old self begins to dissolve, paving the way for a new identity. This process can be likened to the alchemical Philosopher's Stone, symbolizing the goal of transformation and self-realization. During this stage, you start to integrate the lessons learned and crystallize a more authentic self (Jung, 1953). The chaos experienced during this stage is necessary for the transformation, allowing the old to burn away, making space for the new.

Exercise: Transformation

- Identify and challenge limiting beliefs that have held you back. Write them down, then craft affirmations that reflect your emerging self.

- Develop a transformation map outlining the steps you are taking to evolve. Reflect on how each step contributes to your growth and new identity.

The Emergence into Light

The final stage involves emerging from the darkness with renewed clarity and purpose. This phase is characterized by a sense of integration and wholeness as you embrace your true self and prepare to step into a new chapter of life. This mirrors the hero's or heroine's return with the "Elixir," symbolizing the newfound wisdom and transformation (Campbell, 1949). This is a journey back to the self, akin to a return from the waters of Lethe, remembering who you are in this vast universe.

Exercise: Integration and Renewal

- Write a letter to your future self. Describe the insights and strengths you have gained and how you plan to apply them moving forward.

- Set new intentions for your life that align with your renewed purpose. Create actionable goals that reflect this new direction.

Resolution and Integration

Navigating the Dark Night of the Soul requires a combination of self-compassion, reflection, and active engagement with the transformative process.

Here is how to guide yourself through this critical phase:

1. **Embrace the Shadow:**

Confronting and integrating the shadow involves acknowledging and accepting the darker aspects of your psyche, your "shadow factory." This practice fosters greater self-awareness and healing, allowing you to move forward with a more authentic self. Jung refers to this as individuation, a process where the Persona and the Shadow are integrated to uncover the true Self, representing wholeness (Jung, 1953).

Exercise: Shadow Work Journal

- Reflect on recent emotional triggers. What do they reveal about your shadow aspects? How can addressing these insights facilitate your healing process?

- Create a visual representation of your shadow self and explore how it interacts with your conscious identity. This can aid in understanding and integrating these parts of yourself.

2. Seek Meaning and Purpose

A spiritual crisis often accompanies the Dark Night, character-ized by a loss of meaning and purpose. Finding new sources of meaning and purpose can help realign with your core values and passions. This process mirrors the journey of rediscovering paradise after chaos.

Exercise: Values and Purpose Exploration

- Identify your core values and reflect on how they have guid-ed your decisions and actions. How do these values align with your current journey?

- Draft a personal mission statement incorporating your core values and passions. Use this statement to guide your future actions and decisions.

3. Cultivate Self-Compassion

Practicing self-compassion is essential during this period of up-heaval. Be kind to yourself and recognize that growth often in-volves discomfort and challenges.

Exercise: Self-Compassion Practice

- Write a letter to yourself offering understanding and sup-port. Acknowledge your struggles and provide encourage-ment for your journey.

- Engage in mindfulness or meditation practices to cultivate a sense of presence and acceptance. Focus on being present with your emotions and experiences without judgment.

4. Engage in Reflective Practices

Regular reflection supports the integration of insights gained during the Dark Night. Journaling, meditation, and creative ex-pression can help solidify new understandings and facilitate a deeper sense of self.

Exercise: Reflective Journaling

- Dedicate time each day to reflect on your experiences and emotions. Note any shifts in perspective or new insights that arise.

- Explore creative outlets such as art, music, or movement to express your evolving sense of self. These activities can provide additional clarity and understanding.

Dreamwork

To tap into the language of the unconscious for dreamwork, it's helpful to access theta and delta brainwave states, which are associated with deep relaxation and sleep. To reach theta, start with relaxation techniques like deep breathing, progressive muscle relaxation, or gentle meditation. Visualization exercises, where you imagine descending a staircase or floating, can guide the mind toward theta—a frequency common in light sleep and hypnagogic states, where dreams often begin. Dream language isn't literal (words), it's symbolic (images).

For delta waves, which occur in deep, restorative sleep, ensure a calm, distraction-free sleep environment. Practicing mindfulness or guided meditation before sleep can gradually slow your mind and body into these lower frequencies, fostering a deeper connection to dream symbols. Repeating affirmations or setting an intention to remember your dreams can also prime your unconscious, making it easier to tap into its symbolic language upon waking.

Dream journaling immediately after waking is key, as theta and delta insights are often fleeting, yet rich with the subconscious messages you're looking to decode.

Dreamwork can be a powerful exercise for exploring hidden layers of the psyche, unlocking creativity, and finding guidance through the language of symbolic imagery. Start by setting an intention before bed, such as a question or area of life you're seeking clarity on. Keep a dream journal at your bedside to record your dreams as soon as you wake up. In your journal, note any standout symbols, feelings, colors, or characters that appeared.

Reflect on these symbols as if they are facets of your own inner world—are there any figures who represent a particular part of you, such as your wise self or your shadow? Over time, patterns may emerge, revealing recurring themes or insights connected to your identity and aspirations. For deeper understanding, try sketching out your dreams or creating mandalas based on their imagery, connecting to the symbols in a way that bridges your conscious and unconscious selves.

The Path to Wholeness

The Dark Night of the Soul is a profound and transformative phase that challenges you to confront and integrate your shadow aspects. By embracing this process with self-compassion, seeking meaning and purpose, and engaging in reflective practices, you can navigate this period of crisis and emerge with a renewed sense of identity and purpose. This journey mirrors the hero's or heroine's quest for self-discovery.

As we emerge from the depths of the Dark Night of the Soul, we stand at a pivotal moment—where chaos can be transformed into power. This next chapter delves into the transformative power of storytelling and the art of rewriting your narrative. Through this process, you can take the fractured pieces of your past and reassemble them, not as broken, but as facets of a new, sparkling self in **Rewriting Chaos to Victory**. It is here, in the space between suffering and renewal, that the stories of your trauma can be rewritten to reflect your strength, growth, and limitless potential.

CHAPTER 17
REWRITING CHAOS TO VICTORY

Rewriting Trauma: Crystallizing Your Diamond Identity

What if the pain of your past could become the cornerstone of your strength, your wisdom, and your future? What if, like a diamond forged under intense pressure, the deepest wounds you have endured could transform into the brightest facets of your identity? Trauma, while deeply painful, holds the potential to reveal untapped reserves of power, resilience, and creativity. By rewriting your narrative, you do not just heal—you crystallize the dreams and potential you've always held within.

Welcome to Rewriting Trauma, where we embark on a Hero's and Heroine's journey to reclaim our stories and, in turn, ourselves.

Narrative Coaching: Crafting Your Story

Narrative coaching is more than just reflecting on the past. It is an intentional process of revisiting the stories we've lived through, extracting the wisdom, and reframing them to align with who we want to become. Trauma can distort our sense of self, leaving us with fragmented pieces of identity. You will leave the victim behind and embody the energy of a victor. In narrative coaching, we begin to see those fragments not as weaknesses, but as pieces of a powerful mosaic that forms the core of our being.

As we rewrite the narrative, we shift from seeing ourselves as victims of circumstance to creators of our reality. We uncover the diamonds hidden in the rough—those moments of resilience, strength, and courage that have shaped us. In this process, we turn past struggles into future victories, transforming our pain into purpose.

Depth Coaching: Exploring the Shadows

Where narrative coaching reframes our stories, depth coaching dives into the subconscious to explore the layers beneath. This form of coaching invites us to face the shadows, those suppressed emotions and unacknowledged wounds, and understand how they influence our lives. Trauma often buries aspects of our true selves deep within the psyche, but depth coaching brings these hidden facets to the surface.

Working with archetypes like the Hero and Heroine, we explore how these symbolic figures live within us. Often, trauma will suppress either the masculine or feminine aspects of identity, leaving us unbalanced. Depth coaching helps us recognize where we have favored the masculine (drive, competition, independence) or the feminine (nurturing, collaboration, intuition) to survive our trauma. To heal, we need to honor both energies and integrate them fully.

Balancing Feminine and Masculine Identities

For many, trauma involves an imbalance of the masculine and feminine energies within. In a hyper-competitive, trauma-filled environment, we may overemphasize masculine traits like aggressiveness, independence, and control. On the other hand, some of us may over-identify with the feminine, becoming overly nurturing, passive, or self-sacrificing in response to pain.

But the truth is, both energies have vital roles in shaping our identity. Healing requires a balance between the masculine warrior who charges forward with courage and the feminine nurturer who provides compassion and patience. When we can access both sides, we step into a full-spectrum identity that is adaptable, intuitive, strong, and caring. This balance is essential for moving from trauma to empowerment and transforming your professional and personal life.

Male-Dominated Environments and the Glass Ceiling

In many professional settings, particularly in the upper echelons of corporate culture like the C-suite, women face not just external barriers, but a systemic culture that can suppress feminine traits in favor of traditionally masculine ones. The concept of the glass ceiling is not just a metaphor for advancement limits—it symbolizes the deeper, more ingrained societal structures that define power as something male.

In these male-dominated environments, women often feel pressured to conform to masculine ideals: competitiveness, assertiveness, and individualism. While these traits are essential to success in many careers, the suppression of feminine qualities like collaboration, intuition, and emotional intelligence can lead to a fractured identity. When women must downplay their authentic selves to fit into these spaces, they risk disconnecting from their inner wisdom and emotional truth, which can result in burnout, frustration, and an ongoing identity struggle.

The War of Men and Women in the Workplace

The dynamic between men and women in the workplace can be fraught with unspoken tensions. Traditional masculine dominance in leadership roles often means women must fight twice as hard to be seen and heard. Gender bias, microaggressions, and subtle power plays can lead to women feeling marginalized or undervalued.

This war is not always overt; often, it exists in the undercurrents of corporate culture, where men maintain power and control, consciously or unconsciously gatekeeping women from climbing higher in their careers. Women who embrace both their feminine and masculine traits often find themselves stuck between worlds— labeled too "aggressive" if they push forward and too "soft" if they rely on nurturing, empathetic leadership styles.

The War Between Women: Relational Aggression

What complicates this battle even further is the often-unspoken war between women. In many cases, women end up in conflict with one another, not because they inherently wish to compete, but because of systemic structures that pit them against each other for limited spots at the table. This phenomenon, known as relational aggression, manifests as undermining, gossip, exclusion, or passive-aggressive behaviors between women.

Women who have experienced trauma, especially within mother or sister dynamics, may unconsciously reenact these relational wounds in the workplace. The mother wound— which can involve feelings of inadequacy, criticism, or emotional neglect—often plays out in professional environments, where older female mentors may fail to support younger women. Instead of nurturing the next generation of leaders, the cycle of competition and scarcity continues. Similarly, the sister wound—marked by sibling rivalry, jealousy, or betrayal—can show up as distrust or envy between female colleagues.

The result? A cycle of pain, judgment, and division that detracts from the collective power of women in leadership.

Healing the Womb Wound: Reclaiming Power

At the heart of many identity struggles for women lies the womb wound, a deep and primal disconnect from the source of feminine creation and power. This wound symbolizes not just the physical womb, but the metaphorical creative power that women possess. It is the space where intuition, creativity, and nurturing grow, but when this wound is present, women often feel disconnected from their creative potential or feel the need to sacrifice it to survive in masculine environments.

Healing the womb wound involves reclaiming this space as sacred and honoring the feminine essence as equally powerful to the masculine. It requires balancing the desire for professional success with the deep need for authentic self-expression, emotional healing, and creative freedom.

The Hero and Heroine's Journey: A Path to Rebirth

Just as ancient myths depict the Hero's Journey as one of trials, tribulations, and eventual transformation, trauma survivors embark on their own version of this journey. However, we must also consider the Heroine's Journey, which emphasizes not just external conquest, but deep inner healing and integration.

The Hero battles the outer world, but the Heroine heals the inner self, moving through layers of emotional wounding to reclaim her authenticity. Together, the masculine and feminine journeys bring us back to wholeness. Whether you are reclaiming your identity post-military, rebuilding after a toxic work environment, or healing from a personal loss, your journey is one of transformation.

On this journey, each experience—each challenge—polishes the facets of your diamond self, bringing you closer to the highest version of who you can be. Amazing relationships are built when polarity becomes a dance of balance—where opposing forces harmonize in life, love, and career. It's through this dynamic interplay that true connection, passion, and growth flourish. You do not just survive—you crystallize.

Identity: The Diamond with Many Facets

Your identity is like a diamond, multi-faceted, each side reflecting a part of you. Trauma can feel like a crack in that diamond, leaving us feeling broken or diminished. But, just like diamonds are formed under intense pressure, our challenges can carve out new and more brilliant facets within us.

Think of each trauma, wound, or hardship as adding a facet to the diamond of your identity. As you engage in narrative and depth coaching, you begin to recognize that these facets are not imperfections but rather shining facets of your evolving self. The cracks can be healed, polished, and transformed into reflections of your inner strength. Your wounds do not define you—they refine you.

As we journey through life, we often feel as if we are navigating deep space—an infinite void where the stars are distant and the path is uncertain. But it is in this vast expanse, in the silence and mystery of the unknown, that transformation truly begins.

Like diamonds sparkling in the sky, you are the star of your experiences—both light and dark—you are the facets that make up the constellation of your life. Each facet reflects a unique part of you, shaped by challenges, victories, and the IDENTITY GAPS you have encountered. These gaps are not spaces of failure or loss; they are opportunities for growth, for discovering the hidden strengths and values that reside deep within you.

In this guide, we have explored the transformative power of these IDENTITY GAPS and the steps to survive, adapt, and thrive in the void. Just as stars guide space travelers through the darkness, your inner transformation will lead you toward a life of greater purpose and meaning.

You are the astronomer of your journey, the hero of your own story, and the stardust that shines through the challenges of life. You hold the tools to live a life of value, aligning your career and passions with your true self.

As you continue your adventure, remember you are not just surviving the void; you are mastering it, shaping it, and creating a universe where your identity, like the stars, will shine brightly for others to follow. Keep transforming. Keep shining. The universe is waiting for your light.

From Victim to Victor

Transitioning from a victim to a victor is not just about over-coming external challenges—it's about reinventing your identity and embracing the multifaceted nature of who you are. Chaos can shatter your sense of self, leaving you feeling disconnected from your core. However, within that very chaos lies the power to reshape and reclaim your identity, transforming each facet of your being from a source of pain into one of empowerment. When you're caught in the victim mindset, your identity becomes tied to the suffering and limitations that the chaos has imposed. Shifting away from this requires not just healing, but consciously reimagining yourself. The path to becoming a victor starts with redefining how you see yourself in the world, allowing each facet of your identity—your strengths, vulnerabilities, desires, and aspirations—to emerge with renewed clarity.

Reinventing your identity means breaking free from the limitations of your past and embracing the possibility of who you can become. As you navigate through chaos, you gain insight into the various aspects of yourself, rediscovering resilience, creativity, and agency. Each challenge can highlight a different facet of your character, and in embracing those facets, you step into your power. Victory is not just about overcoming—it's about reclaiming your wholeness. By rewriting your story, you transform chaos into a tool for growth, and each part of your identity becomes a testament to your journey from victimhood to victory.

As earthlings, we are all travelers in an ever-shifting universe of change and possibility. The void, vast and endless, can feel disorienting—like floating in space without a tether, unsure of where to anchor. But within this void lies an opportunity to discover the facets of your true self, to explore the depths of your identity as if you were an astronaut charting new constellations in uncharted galaxies.

Your IDENTITY GAP may feel like a black hole, pulling at the edges of who you thought you were. But even within this cosmic uncertainty, there is light. Each challenge, transition, or moment of chaos is a starburst—a chance to see yourself from a different angle, revealing the brilliance of the diamond within you. Like the planets orbiting the sun, the facets of your identity— your strengths, fears, desires, and dreams—come into alignment through the gravitational pull of self-discovery.

Moving from chaos to victory means embracing the journey through the void. It's in the void that you are free to reinvent your identity, to navigate through the vastness of possibility. The spaces where you feel lost are the very places that give you room to grow, allowing you to refine each part of yourself until you emerge shining like a diamond—a multifaceted, resilient being ready to face new horizons.

In the end, surviving the void isn't about escaping it. It's about realizing that you are the star. Your identity, forged in the fires of challenge and discovery, is the compass that will always guide you. No matter how vast the void seems, you have the tools to navigate it, reclaim your power, and shine as bright as any galaxy.

Final Thoughts: The Challenge of Victory

It was challenging enough to get out of the IDENTITY GAP and reinvent yourself, but now nobody knows you, and it's like you're a martian to them. You've fought your battles, faced your fears, and emerged victorious—a transformed person. But when you return home, you realize something unexpected: the people who knew you before aren't celebrating your growth. Instead, they seem to want the old you back, the person they're comfortable with. Why does this happen?

The truth is, when we evolve, we often disrupt the roles and dynamics that others have grown used to. Friends, family, and colleagues may subconsciously resist your change because it forces them to confront their own stagnation or insecurities. It's not that they don't care about you; it's that your transformation highlights what they haven't changed in themselves. This can feel isolating, as though you're straddling two worlds—the one you've outgrown and the one you're striving toward.

How do you overcome this?

1. **Own Your Growth**: You've done the challenging work to transform. Don't diminish your accomplishments to fit into others' expectations. Embrace who you've become, even if it makes others uncomfortable.

2. **Communicate Openly**: Share your journey with the people who matter. Let them know why you've changed and how this updated version of yourself is more aligned with your truth.

3. **Create New Boundaries**: Sometimes, you'll need to set boundaries with those who insist on pulling you back. It's essential to protect your progress and not allow others to derail your growth.

4. **Surround Yourself with Growth-Minded People**: Don't fall back into old stories and an old identity. Seek out individuals who encourage and support your transformation. The right environment is critical for continued evolution.

Returning home changed can be challenging, but remember, you've already proven your strength on the journey. Now, the challenge is staying true to who you've become.

Welcome to your victory—where the universe of your identity awaits your next adventure.

Martian (in a soft tone): "Bleep, bleep… IDENTITY GAP closed. Mission accomplished."

Human (with a smile of relief): "Yeah, mission accomplished… for now. Until the next adventure."

RESEARCH

CHAPTER 1

- Atanasov AG, Yeung AWK, Klager E, Eibensteiner F, Schaden E, Kletecka-Pulker M, Willschke H. First, Do No Harm (Gone Wrong): Total-Scale Analysis of Medical Errors Scientific Literature. Front Public Health. 2020 Oct 16;8:558913. doi: 10.3389/fpubh.2020.558913. PMID: 33178657; PM-CID: PMC7596242.

CHAPTER 2

- AARP Foundation. (2020). The Pandemic Effect: A Social Isolation Report. Retrieved from AARP Foundation.

- Baumeister, R. F., & Leary, M. R. (1995). "The Need to Belong: Desire for Interpersonal Attachments as a Fundamental Human Motivation." Psychological Bulletin, 117(3), 497-529.

- Blue Zones Research (2020): Studies of the world's longest-living populations, known as "Blue Zones," reveal that having a strong sense of purpose, referred to as "ikigai" in Japan or "plan de vida" in Costa Rica, is associated with longer life expectancy. People who identify a clear purpose in life can add up to seven years to their lives.

- Brown, C., & Lee, H. (2022). Navigating Life Transitions

- Charmaz, K. (1983). Loss of Self: A Fundamental Form of Suffering in the Chronically Ill. Sociology of Health & Illness, 5(2), 168-195. doi:10.1111/1467-9566.ep10491512

- Erikson, E. H. (1950). Childhood and Society. W.W. Norton & Company.

- Erikson, E. H. (1968). Identity: Youth and Crisis. Norton.

- Farmer, M. E., Locke, B. Z., Moscicki, E. K., Dannenberg, A. L., Larson, D. B., & Radloff, L. S. (1988). "Physical Activity and Depressive Symptoms: The NHANES I Epidemiologic Follow-Up Study." American Journal of Epidemiology, 128(6), 1340-1351.

- Gallup Well-Being Index (2021): According to Gallup, individuals who strongly agree that they have a clear purpose in life are 2.5 times more likely to report being "thriving" in their overall well-being compared to those who do not.

- Ginzburg, K., & Michaeli, N. (2016). Role Discontinuity, Transition, and the Experience of Loss in Retirement.

- Ibarra, H. (2004). Working Identity: Unconventional Strategies for Reinventing Your Career.

- James, W. (1890). The Principles of Psychology. Henry Holt and Company.

- Luyckx, K., Schwartz, S. J., Goossens, L., & Pollock, S. (2008). "Identity Processes and Coping Strategies in Adolescence: Associations with Developmental Transitions and Future Considerations." Developmental Psychology, 44(4), 1023-1039.

- Marcia, J. E. (1980). Identity in Adolescence. In J. Adelson (Ed.), Handbook of Adolescent Psychology. Wiley.

- Maslach, C., & Leiter, M. P. (2016). Understanding the Burnout Experience.

- Mayo Clinic. (2021). Empty Nest Syndrome: Tips for Coping. Retrieved from Mayo Clinic Website

- McAdams, D. P. (2001). The Psychology of Life Stories. Review of General Psychology.

- Mead, G. H. (1934). Mind, Self, and Society: From the Standpoint of a Social Behaviorist. University of Chicago Press.

- Neff, K. D. (2003). Self-Compassion: An Alternative Conceptualization of a Healthy Attitude Toward Oneself. Self and Identity.

- Pinquart, M. (2002). Creating and Maintaining Purpose in Life in Old Age: A Meta-Analysis. Journal of Aging Studies, 16(3), 217-242. doi:10.1016/S0890-4065(02)00054-2

- Rogers, C. R. (1961). On Becoming a Person: A Therapist's View of Psychotherapy. Houghton Mifflin Harcourt.

- Schwartz, S. J., Klimstra, T. A., Luyckx, K., Hale, W. W., & Meeus, W. H. (2012). "Characterizing the Self-System over Time in Adolescence: Internal Structure and Associations with Internalizing Symptoms." Journal of Youth and Adolescence, 41(9), 1208-1221.

- Schwartz, S. J., Luyckx, K., & Vignoles, V. L. (2011). Handbook of Identity Theory and Research. Springer.

- Erikson, E. H. (1950). Childhood and Society. W. W. Norton & Company.

- Schwartz, S. J., Zamboanga, B. L., Weisskirch, R. S., & Rodriguez, L. (2009). "The Relationships of Personal and Cultural Identity to Adaptive and Maladaptive Psychosocial Functioning in Emerging Adults." Journal of Social Psychology, 149(5), 515-540.

- Smith, A., & Johnson, T. (2023). The State of Identity Crisis: Statistical Insights. Journal of Personal Development.

- Super, D. E. (1980). A Life-Span, Life-Space Approach to Career Development.

- Tajfel, H., & Turner, J. C. (1986). The Social Identity Theory of Intergroup Behavior.

- Turner, J. C., Hogg, M. A., Oakes, P. J., Reicher, S. D., & Wetherell, M. S. (1987). Rediscovering the Social Group: A Self-Categorization Theory.

- Twenge, J. M., & Campbell, W. K. (2009). The Narcissism Epidemic: Living in the Age of Entitlement. Free Press.

- Vignoles, V. L., Schwartz, S. J., & Luyckx, K. (2011). Handbook of Identity Theory and Research. Springer.

- Wang, M., & Shultz, K. S. (2010). Employee Retirement: A Review and Recommendations for Future Investigation. Journal of Management, 36(1), 172-206. doi:10.1177/0149206309347957

- Waterman, A. S. (1993). "Developmental Perspectives on Identity Formation: From Adolescence to Adulthood." In J. Kroger (Ed.), Discussions on Ego Identity. Lawrence Erlbaum Associates.

- World Health Organization. (2017). Mental Health of Older Adults. Retrieved from WHO.

CHAPTER 3

- Brown, B. (2015). Rising Strong: How the Ability to Reset Transforms the Way We Live, Love, Parent, and Lead. Spiegel & Grau.

- Csikszentmihalyi, M. (1990). Flow: The Psychology of Optimal Experience. Harper & Row.

- Duckworth, A. (2016). Grit: The Power of Passion and Perseverance. Scribner.

- Dweck, C. S. (2006). Mindset: The New Psychology of Success. Random House.

- Seligman, M. E. P. (2006). Learned Optimism: How to Change Your Mind and Your Life. Vintage.

CHAPTER 4

- American Psychological Association. "Grief." APA.

- Carr, D., & Utz, R. L. (2020). Late-Life Widowhood in the United States: New Directions in Research and Theory. Ageing & Society, 40(9), 1876-1906. doi:10.1017/S0144686X19000089

- HeartMath Institute. The HeartMath Solution: The Institute of HeartMath's Revolutionary Program for Engaging the Power of the Heart's Intelligence. HarperOne, 1999.

- Kübler-Ross, Elisabeth. On Death and Dying. Scribner, 1997.

- Worden, J. William. Grief Counseling and Grief Therapy: A Handbook for the Mental Health Practitioner. Springer Publishing Company, 2018.

CHAPTER 5

- Ben-Shahar, Tal. Ph.D. (2007). Happier: Learn the Secrets to Daily Joy and Lasting Fulfillment. McGraw-Hill.

- Boyle, P. A., Buchman, A. S., Barnes, L. L., & Bennett, D. A. (2010). Effect of a Purpose in Life on Risk of Incident Alzheimer Disease and Mild Cognitive Impairment in Community-Dwelling Older Persons. Archives of General Psychiatry, 67(3), 304-310. doi:10.1001/archgenpsychiatry.2009.208

- Bridges, W. (2004). Transitions: Making Sense of Life's Changes. Da Capo Press.

- Brown, B. (2015). Rising Strong: How the Ability to Reset Transforms the Way We Live, Love, Parent, and Lead. Spiegel & Grau.

- Burnett, Bill, and Dave Evans. Designing Your Life: How to Build a Well-Lived, Joyful Life. Knopf, 2016.

- Clear, J. (2018). Atomic Habits: An Easy & Proven Way to Build Good Habits & Break Bad Ones. Avery.

- Clifton, Donald O., and Edward "Chip" Anderson. StrengthsQuest: Discover and Develop Your Strengths in Academics, Career, and Beyond. Gallup Press, 2002.

- Csikszentmihalyi, Mihaly. Flow: The Psychology of Optimal Experience. Harper & Row, 1990.

- Duckworth, A. (2016). Grit: The Power of Passion and Perseverance. Scribner.

- Dweck, C. S. (2006). Mindset: The New Psychology of Success. Random House.

- Erikson, E. H. (1968). Identity: Youth and Crisis. W. W. Norton & Company.

- Gallup. (2019). State of the Global Workplace: 2019 Report. Gallup Press.

- Herzberg, F. (1966). Work and the Nature of Man. World Publishing Company.

- Hill, P. L., & Turiano, N. A. (2014). Purpose in Life as a Predictor of Mortality Across Adulthood. Psychological Science, 25(7), 1482-1486. doi:10.1177/0956797614531799

- Ibarra, H. (2004). Working Identity: Unconventional Strategies for Reinventing Your Career. Harvard Business Review Press.

- Kim, E. S., Sun, J. K., Park, N., & Peterson, C. (2013). Purpose in Life and Reduced Incidence of Stroke in Older Adults: 'The Health and Retirement Study'. Journal of Psychosomatic Research, 74(5), 427-432. doi:10.1016/j. jpsychores.2013.02.013

- Markus, H., & Ruvolo, A. (1989). Possible Selves: Personalized Representations of Goals. In L. A. Pervin (Ed.), Goal Concepts in Personality and Social Psychology (pp. 211-241). Erlbaum.

- Maslow, A. H. (1943). A Theory of Human Motivation. Psychological Review, 50(4), 370-396.

- Myers, Isabel Briggs, and Peter B. Myers. Gifts Differing: Understanding Personality Type. Davies-Black Publishing, 1995.

- Oyserman, D., Bybee, D., & Terry, K. (2006). Possible Selves and Academic Outcomes: How and When Possible Selves Impel Action. Journal of Personality and Social Psychology, 91(1), 188-204.

- Rokeach, M. (1973). The Nature of Human Values. Free Press.

- Ryff, C. D., & Keyes, C. L. M. (1995). The Structure of Psychological Well-Being Revisited. Journal of Personality and Social Psychology, 69(4), 719-727. doi:10.1037/0022-3514.69.4.719

- Schlossberg, N. K. (2011). Revitalizing Retirement: Reshaping Your Identity, Relationships, and Purpose. American Psychological Association.

- Schwartz, S. H. (1992). Universals in the Content and Structure of Values: Theoretical Advances and Empirical Tests in 20 Countries. Advances in Experimental Social Psychology, 25, 1-65.

- Seligman, M. E. P. (2006). Learned Optimism: How to Change Your Mind and Your Life. Vintage.

- Spencer, H. (2014). Who Moved My Cheese? An A-Mazing Way to Deal with Change in Your Work and in Your Life. Putnam Adult.

- Steger, M. F., Oishi, S., & Kashdan, T. B. (2009). Meaning in Life Across the Life Span: Levels and Correlates of Meaning in Life from Emerging Adulthood to Older Adulthood. Journal of Positive Psychology, 4(1), 43-52. doi:10.1080/17439760802303127

- Up to 55% of our occupational identity is derived from our work (Smith, 2023).

- Wrzesniewski, A., McCauley, C., Rozin, P., & Schwartz, B. (1997). Jobs, Careers, and Callings: People's Relations to Their Work. Journal of Research in Personality, 31(1), 21-33. doi:10.1006/jrpe.1997.2162

- Zika, S., & Chamberlain, K. (1992). On the Relation Between Meaning in Life and Psychological Well-being. British Journal of Psychology, 83(1), 133-145. doi:10.1111/j.2044-8295.1992.tb02429.x

CHAPTER 6

- Aaker, D. (2010). Brand Relevance: Making Competitors Irrelevant. Jossey-Bass.

- Arruda, W., & Dixson, K. (2007). Career Distinction: Stand Out by Building Your Brand. John Wiley & Sons.

- Clark, D. (2015). Stand Out: How to Find Your Breakthrough Idea and Build a Following Around It. Portfolio.

- Clear, J. (2018). Atomic Habits: An Easy & Proven Way to Build Good Habits & Break Bad Ones. Penguin Random House.

- Erdogan, B. Z., & Baker, M. J. (2000). "Celebrity Endorsement: A Literature Review." Journal of Marketing Management, 16(7), 291-314.

- Jung, C. G. (1959). The Archetypes and the Collective Unconscious. Princeton University Press.

- Jung, Carl. The Archetypes and the Collective Unconscious. Princeton University Press, 1981.

- Kaputa, C. (2012). You Are a Brand!: In Person and Online, How Smart People Brand Themselves for Business Success. Nicholas Brealey Publishing.

- Keller, K. L. (2012). Strategic Brand Management: Building, Measuring, and Managing Brand Equity. Pearson.

- Labrecque, L. I., Markos, E., & Milne, G. R. (2011). "Online Personal Branding: Processes, Challenges, and Implications." Journal of Interactive Marketing, 25(1), 37-50.

- Mark, Margaret, and Carol S. Pearson. The Hero and the Outlaw: Building Extraordinary Brands Through the Power of Archetypes. McGraw-Hill, 2001.

- McNally, D., & Speak, K. D. (2011). Be Your Own Brand: Achieve More of What You Want by Being More of Who You Are. Berrett-Koehler Publishers.

- Montoya, P., & Vandehey, T. (2008). The Brand Called You: Make Your Business Stand Out in a Crowded Marketplace. McGraw-Hill Education.

- Neumeier, M. (2006). The Brand Gap: How to Bridge the Distance Between Business Strategy and Design. New Riders.

- Peters, T. (1997). "The Brand Called You." Fast Company.

- Rao, V. R., Agarwal, M. K., & Dahlhoff, D. (2004). "How Is Manifest Branding Strategy Related to the Intangible Value of a Corporation?" Journal of Marketing, 68(4), 126-141.

- Ries, A., & Trout, J. (1981). Positioning: The Battle for Your Mind. McGraw-Hill.

CHAPTER 7

- Bradshaw, John. (1995). Healing the Shame that Binds You. Health Communications. This book discusses the effects of shame and narcissistic abuse on self-identity and recovery strategies.

- Brock, William H. (2020). The Hero's Journey in Trauma Recovery: Exploring the Process of Transformation. Journal of Psychotherapy Integration, 30(2), 139-155.

- Frankl, V. E. (2006). Man's Search for Meaning. Boston: Beacon Press.

- Frankl, Viktor E. Man's Search for Meaning. Beacon Press, 2006.

- Goldsmith, Marshall, & Reiter, Alan. (2007). What Got You Here Won't Get You There: How Successful People Become Even More Successful. Hyperion. This book explores the challenges and opportunities for growth in times of change and chaos.

- Herman, J. L. (1992). Trauma and Recovery: The Aftermath of Violence—From Domestic Abuse to Political Terror. New York: Basic Books.

- Jones, R., & Taylor, M. (2022). The Psychological Effects of Unemployment and Underemployment. Employment and Mental Health Review.

- Maslach, C., & Leiter, M. P. (2016). Burnout: A Brief History and How to Measure It. In T. Fisher (Ed.), Workplace Burnout: A Comprehensive Overview. New York: WorkLife Press.

- Maslach, C., Schaufeli, W. B., & Leiter, M. P. (2001). Job Burnout. Annual Review of Psychology, 52, 397-422.

- Miller, A. (1997). The Drama of the Gifted Child: The Search for the True Self. New York: Basic Books.

- Neff, Kristen. (2011). Self-Compassion: The Proven Power of Being Kind to Yourself.

- Parker, William M. (2019). Navigating Moral Injury: Understanding and Managing the Emotional and Psychological Impact of Ethical Violations. Ethics & Behavior, 29(4), 297-311. This article addresses the concept of moral injury and its effect on personal identity.

- Smith, A. (2023). Occupational Identity and Its Impact on Well-being. Journal of Occupational Psychology.

- Tischler, Barbara. (2014). The Effects of Narcissistic Abuse on the Sense of Self. Journal of Clinical Psychology, 70(5), 477-490. Tischler's research investigates the impact of narcissistic abuse on self-identity and recovery.

- Van Der Kolk, B. (2015). The Body Keeps the Score: Brain, Mind, and Body in the Healing of Trauma. New York: Viking.

- Walker, P. (2013). Complex PTSD: From Surviving to Thriving. Vallejo, CA: Azure Coyote Publishing. Bottom of Form

- White, L., & Green, P. (2021). Adjusting to Disability: Identity and Career Transition. Journal of Disability Studies.

CHAPTER 8

- Beard, M. (2017). Women & Power: A Manifesto. Liveright Publishing.

- Bourdieu, P. (1984). Distinction: A Social Critique of the Judgment of Taste. Harvard University Press.

- Gilligan, C. (1982). In a Different Voice: Psychological Theory and Women's Development. Harvard University Press.

- Hochschild, A. R., & Machung, A. (2012). The Second Shift: Working Families and the Revolution at Home. Penguin Books.

- National Center for Women & Veterans' Health. (2021). Women Veterans Health Care. Retrieved from VA Website

- Women Veterans Alliance. (2023). About Us. Retrieved from Women Veterans Alliance

- Yousafzai, M., & Lamb, C. (2013). I Am Malala: The Girl Who Stood Up for Education and Was Shot by the Taliban. Little, Brown, and Company.

CHAPTER 9

- Aurelius, M. (2002). Meditations. Dover Publications.

- Aurelius, M. (2002). Meditations. Translated by Gregory Hays. Modern Library.

- Epictetus. (2008). Discourses and Selected Writings. Penguin Classics.

- Epictetus. (2008). The Enchiridion. Digireads.com Publishing.

- Irvine, W. B. (2008). A Guide to the Good Life: The Ancient Art of Stoic Joy. Oxford University Press.

- Murdock, Maureen. (1990). The Heroine's Journey: Woman's Quest for Wholeness. Shambhala Publications.

- Seneca, L. A. (2004). Letters from a Stoic. Dover Publications.

- Seneca, L.A. (2008). Letters from a Stoic. Penguin Classics.

- Le Guin, Ursula K. (1989). The Language of the Night: Essays on Fantasy and Science Fiction. Berkley Books.

CHAPTER 10

- Chan, W. (2010). The Tao of Wisdom: The Wisdom of Lao Tzu and Confucius. Inner Traditions.

- Irvine, W. B. (2008). A Guide to the Good Life: The Ancient Art of Stoic Joy. Oxford University Press.

- Jung, C. G. (1961). Psychological Aspects of the Persona. Princeton University Press.

- Kumar, K. (2011). The Dance of Shiva and Shakti: The Meaning and Impact of the Divine Feminine and Masculine Energies. HarperCollins.

- Kumar, S. (2011). The Power of Shakti: Awakening the Energy of the Divine Feminine. HarperOne.

- Miller, J. B. (2016). The Drama of the Gifted Child: The Search for the True Self. Basic Books.

CHAPTER 11

- Coll, J. E., Weiss, E. L., & Yarvis, J. S. (2011). The impact of military culture on mental health in the military. Military Medicine, 176(8), 382-387.

- Employment and the IDENTITY GAP in Veteran Transitions," Institute for Veterans and Military Families.

- Hall, L. K. (2011). The importance of understanding military culture. Social Work in Health Care, 50(1), 4-18.

- Iverson, K. M., King, M. W., Cunningham, K. C., Resick, P. A., Gerber, M. R., Kimerling, R., & Vogt, D. (2015). Rationale, design, and methods of a study examining gender differences in intimate partner violence and mental health among Iraq and Afghanistan Veterans. Contemporary Clinical Trials, 45, 100-108.

- Maury, R., Stone, B., & Roseman, E. (2014). Veteran Social Reintegration Study. University of Southern California. Retrieved from CIR.

- Mental Health Challenges in Veterans During Transition," Journal of Anxiety Disorders.

- Office of Public Health. (2013). Post-Deployment Health: Suicide among Veterans. U.S. Department of Veterans Affairs. Retrieved from VA.gov

- Orazem, R. J., Frazier, P. A., Schnurr, P. P., Oleson, H. E., Carlson, K. F., & Litz, B. T. (2017). Identity adjustment among Afghanistan and Iraq war veterans with reintegration difficulty. Psychological Trauma: Theory, Research, Practice, and Policy, 9(1), 4–11.

- Pew Research Center. (2011). The Difficult Transition from Military to Civilian Life. Retrieved from Pew Research Center

- Tanielian, T., & Jaycox, L. H. (Eds.). (2008). Invisible Wounds of War: Psychological and Cognitive Injuries, Their Consequences, and Services to Assist Recovery. RAND Corporation. doi:10.7249/MG720

- The U.S. Department of Veterans Affairs (2021) reported that the suicide rate among veterans is 1.5 times higher than that of the general population. Identity struggles, including the loss of a military identity and difficulty in finding a new purpose, are significant contributing factors.

- U.S. Bureau of Labor Statistics. (2021). Employment Situation of Veterans – 2021. Retrieved from BLS.gov

- U.S. Department of Veterans Affairs. (2021). National Veteran Suicide Prevention Annual Report. Retrieved from VA.gov

- Vest, B. M., Kulak, J. A., Hall, V. M., & Wallace, A. E. (2019). Transitioning from Military to Civilian Life: Examining Identity Issues in Veterans. Journal of Veterans Studies, 5(1), 34-46. doi:10.21061/jvs.v5i1.93

- Veterans' Struggles with Civilian Life: The Impact of Loss of Structure," Journal of Clinical Psychology.

- Westwood, M. J., Black, T. G., & McLean, H. B. (2002). A Re-entry Program for Peacekeepers Coming Home. Canadian Journal of Counselling, 36(3), 221-232.

CHAPTER 12

- Bowlby, J. (1988). A Secure Base: Parent-Child Attachment and Healthy Human Development. Basic Books.

- Bradshaw, J. (1990). Homecoming: Reclaiming and Championing Your Inner Child. Health Communications.

- Dreikurs, R. (2007). The Psychology of Interpersonal Relations. Kessinger Publishing.

- Gottlieb, L. (2017). Maybe You Should Talk to Someone: A Therapist, HER Therapist, and Our Lives Revealed. Houghton Mifflin Harcourt.

- Jung, C. G. (1953). Psychological Aspects of the Persona. Princeton University Press.

- Lad, V. (2016). The Way of Women: Awakening Our Sexuality, Healing Our Spirits. Inner Traditions.

- Nicol, L. (2019). The Mother Wound: How to Heal and Embrace Your Authentic Self. New World Library.

CHAPTER 13

- American Psychiatric Association. Diagnostic and Statistical Manual of Mental Disorders (DSM-5). American Psychiatric Association Publishing, 2013.

- Bowlby, J. (1988). A Secure Base: Parent-Child Attachment and Healthy Human Development. Routledge.

- Bradshaw, J. (2013). Healing the Shame That Binds You. Health Communications, Inc.

- Bushman, Brad J., and Roy F. Baumeister. "Threatened Egotism, Narcissism, Self-Esteem, and Direct and Displaced Aggression: Does Self-Love or Self-Hate Lead to Violence?" Journal of Personality and Social Psychology, vol. 75, no. 1, 1998, pp. 219-229.

- Buss, David M., and Todd K. Shackelford. "Human Aggression in Evolutionary Psychological Perspective." Clinical Psychology Review, vol. 17, no. 6, 1997, pp. 605-619.

- Campbell, W. Keith, and Jean M. Twenge. The Narcissism Epidemic: Living in the Age of Entitlement. Free Press, 2009.

- Crick, Nicki R., and Jennifer K. Grotpeter. "Relational Aggression, Gender, and Social-Psychological Adjustment." Child Development, vol. 66, no. 3, 1995, pp. 710-722.

- Dellasega, Cheryl. Mean Girls Grown Up: Adult Women Who Are Still Queen Bees, Middle Bees, and Afraid-to-Bees. Wiley, 2005.

- Drexler, Peggy. "Why Women Don't Support Other Women." The Wall Street Journal, 2013.

- Eagly, Alice H., and Linda L. Carli. Through the Labyrinth: The Truth About How Women Become Leaders. Harvard Business Review Press, 2007.

- Glick, Peter, et al. "Beyond Prejudice as Simple Antipathy: Hostile and Benevolent Sexism Across Cultures." Journal of Personality and Social Psychology, vol. 79, no. 5, 2000, pp. 763-775.

- Kernberg, Otto F. Aggression in Personality Disorders and Perversions. Yale University Press, 1992.

- Kernberg, Otto F. Borderline Conditions and Pathological Narcissism. Jason Aronson, 1975.

- Kjærvik, Sarah L., and David DeSteno. The Interpersonal Consequences of Narcissism: A Review and a Preliminary Model." Frontiers in Psychology, vol. 9, 2018, article 39.

- Masterson, James F. The Narcissistic and Borderline Disorders: An Integrated Developmental Approach. Routledge, 1981.

- Millon, Theodore, and Roger D. Davis. Personality Disorders in Modern Life. John Wiley & Sons, 1996.

- Morf, Carolyn C., and Frederick Rhodewalt. "Unraveling the Paradoxes of Narcissism: A Dynamic Self-Regulatory Processing Model." Psychological Inquiry, vol. 12, no. 4, 2001, pp. 177-196.

- Riso, D. R., & Hudson, R. (1999). The Wisdom of the Enneagram: The Complete Guide to Psychological and Spiritual Growth for the Nine Personality Types. Bantam.

- Ronningstam, Elsa. Identifying and Understanding the Narcissistic Personality. Oxford University Press, 2005.

- Sandberg, Sheryl. Lean In: Women, Work, and the Will to Lead. Knopf, 2013.

- Shinoda Bolen, J. (1994). The Power of the Crone: Myths and Stories of the Wise Woman Archetype. HarperOne.

- Singer, J. (1994). The Wounded Woman: Healing the Father-Daughter Relationship. Shambhala.

- Twenge, Jean M. Generation Me: Why Today's Young Americans Are More Confident, Assertive, Entitled—and More Miserable Than Ever Before. Free Press, 2006.

- Twenge, Jean M., and W. Keith Campbell. Narcissism and the Challenge of Self-Love in Contemporary Society. Palgrave Macmillan, 2016.

- Twenge, Jean M., and W. Keith Campbell. The Narcissism Epidemic: Living in the Age of Entitlement. Free Press, 2009.

- Underwood, Marion K. Social Aggression among Girls. Guilford Press, 2003.

- Walker, P. (2013). Complex PTSD: From Surviving to Thriving: A Guide and Map for Recovering from Childhood Trauma. Azure Coyote Publishing.

- Weinhold, J., & Weinhold, B. (2010). The Flight from Intimacy: Healing Your Relationship of Counter-dependency. New World Library.

- Wiseman, Rosalind. Queen Bees and Wannabes: Helping Your Daughter Survive Cliques, Gossip, Boyfriends, and Other Realities of Adolescence. Three Rivers Press, 2009.

- Wood, J., & Altman, H. (2015). The Father Wound: How Your Father's Lack of Affirmation May Affect Your Adult Relationships and What You Can Do About It. Hope For Your Heart.

CHAPTER 14

- Brown, Brené. Daring Greatly: How the Courage to Be Vulnerable Transforms the Way We Live, Love, Parent, and Lead. Gotham Books, 2012.

- Chua, Amy. Battle Hymn of the Tiger Mother. Penguin Press, 2011.

- Eagly, Alice H., and Linda L. Carli. Through the Labyrinth: The Truth About How Women Become Leaders. Harvard Business Review Press, 2007.

- Sandberg, Sheryl. Lean In: Women, Work, and the Will to Lead. Knopf, 2013.

- Twenge, Jean M. Generation Me: Why Today's Young Americans Are More Confident, Assertive, Entitled—and More Miserable Than Ever Before. Free Press, 2006.

CHAPTER 15

- Campbell, J. (1949). *The Hero with a Thousand Faces*. Princeton University Press.

- Jung, C. G. (1953). Collected Works of C.G. Jung, Volume 12: *Psychology and Alchemy*. Princeton University Press.

- Jung, C. G. (1953). Collected Works of C.G. Jung, Volume 9 (Part 1): *The Archetypes and The Collective Unconscious*. Princeton University Press.

- Jung, C. G. (1961). *Memories, Dreams, Reflections*. Pantheon Books.

- May, G. G. (2004). *The Dark Night of the Soul: A Psychiatrist Explores the Connection Between Darkness and Spiritual Growth*. HarperOne.

- Moore, T. (1992). *Care of the Soul: A Guide for Cultivating Depth and Sacredness in Everyday Life*. HarperCollins.

- Peck, M. S. (1978). *The Road Less Traveled: A New Psychology of Love, Traditional Values, and Spiritual Growth*. Simon & Schuster.

- Rohr, R. (2002). *Everything Belongs: The Gift of Contemplative Prayer*. Crossroad Publishing Company.

- Saint John of the Cross. (1577). The Dark Night of the Soul.

- Underhill, E. (1911). *Mysticism: A Study in the Nature and Development of Spiritual Consciousness*. E.P. Dutton & Co.

- Vaughan-Lee, L. (1995). *The Call and the Echo: Sufi Dreamwork and the Psychology of the Beloved*. The Golden Sufi Center.

CHAPTER 16

- Brené Brown - *The Gifts of Imperfection: Let Go of Who You Think You're Supposed to Be and Embrace Who You Are*. Hazelden Publishing, 2010.

- Carl G. Jung - *The Archetypes and the Collective Unconscious.* Princeton University Press, 1959.Dan P. McAdams - *The Stories We Live By: Personal Myths and the Making of the Self.* The Guilford Press, 1993.

- Joseph Campbell - *The Hero with a Thousand Faces.* Pantheon Books, 1949.Clarissa Pinkola Estés - *Women Who Run with the Wolves: Myths and Stories of the Wild Woman Archetype.* Ballantine Books, 1992.

- Marion Woodman - *Leaving My Father's House: A Journey to Conscious Femininity.* Shambhala Publications, 1992.

- Patricia Evans - *The Verbally Abusive Relationship: How to Recognize It and How to Respond.* Adams Media, 1996.

- Robert Bly - *Iron John: A Book About Men.* Addison-Wesley, 1990.

www.ingramcontent.com/pod-product-compliance
Lightning Source LLC
Chambersburg PA
CBHW060139150626
46550CB00015B/1905